Microcomputers in
Education

By the same author (with Tim O'Shea)

Learning and Teaching with Computers, Harvester Press, 1983

Microcomputers in Education

A Critical Evaluation of Educational Software

JOHN SELF
Lecturer in Computing
University of Lancaster

HARVESTER
PRESS
1970 1985
FIFTEEN
FORWARD-LOOKING
YEARS

THE HARVESTER PRESS

First published in Great Britain in 1985 by
THE HARVESTER PRESS LIMITED
Publisher: John Spiers
16 Ship Street, Brighton, Sussex

© John Self, 1985

British Library Cataloguing in Publication Data

Self, John
  Microcomputers in education.
  1. Computer-assisted instruction
  2. Microcomputers
  I. Title
  370'.28'5404   LB1028.5

  ISBN 0-7108-0936-0
  ISBN 0-7108-0946-8 Pbk

Typeset in 11 point Bembo by
Photobooks (Bristol) Ltd
Printed in Great Britain by
Whitstable Litho Ltd., Whitstable, Kent

THE HARVESTER PRESS PUBLISHING GROUP
The Harvester Press Publishing Group comprises Harvester Press
Limited (chiefly publishing literature, fiction, philosophy,
psychology, and science and trade books), Harvester Press
Microform Publications Limited (publishing in microform
unpublished archives, scarce printed sources, and indexes to these
collections) and Wheatsheaf Books Limited (a wholly independent
company chiefly publishing in economics, international politics,
sociology and related social sciences), whose books are distributed
by The Harvester Press Limited and its agencies throughout the
world.

Contents

Preface

The quantity of educational software is growing alarmingly—and I do mean alarmingly. For while the number of computers in education, and in consequence the software for them, has expanded remarkably since 1980, the quality of most of this software is lacking. Most unbiased observers would agree with this opinion. This book goes further in arguing that not only is present educational software poor but that, if present design strategies continue to be followed, there is little prospect of an improvement. The transient difficulties of today are masking much deeper problems that have yet to be faced. This book, then, is an attempt to provide a critical assessment of the prospects for educational software development.

Nobody can fail to be impressed by the hard-working dedication and missionary fervour of those involved in educational computing today. However, I have come to feel that much of this effort is misplaced. I can only hope that the criticisms in this book will be taken as they are intended; that is, as an attempt to steer these efforts into more fruitful avenues. Several readers have commented that they found the message of this book rather depressing. This is good, for it is time that we questioned the aura of inherent worthiness which has surrounded computers in education.

The book is intended for teachers, parents and planners concerned with educational computing, but not necessarily trained in either computing or educational psychology. More specifically, the book is aimed at those who may design and develop educational software in the future.

My view of the educational computing scene took shape during a year spent helping the Open University prepare a course on Educational Software as part of a Micros in Schools project funded by the Microelectronics Education Programme. I am very grateful to the Open University for providing this opportunity, and especially to the members of the P541 course team: John Jaworski, Ann Jones, Dave Perry, Jenny Preece and Malcolm Story. I am grateful also to the many individuals outside the Open University who gave generously of their time. I would also like to thank the following for reading and commenting upon a draft of this book: Mike Brooke, Iain Craig, Terry Horne, Harry Lewis, Tim O'Shea, Jim Ridgway, Ruth Self, David Smith and Ken Tait. Of course, none of the above should be considered to endorse any of the opinions expressed in this book or to be responsible for any errors of fact.

Like all books concerning new technology, this one runs the risk of being out-of-date before it reaches the bookshops. There will be new computers and new programs by then, but I doubt that the quality of educational software will have radically altered. I shall be delighted when the message of this book becomes out-of-date.

Global declaration: In the following pages, 'he' stands for 'he/she' and 'his' for 'his/her'.

PART 1

Introduction

Part 1 begins with a transcript of a 'typical' classroom lesson using a representative educational software package. This is followed in Chapter 2 by a detailed critique of this one program, which is intended to provide a context for the following discussion. Chapter 3 begins with an explanation of the aims and organisation of the rest of the book. I then try to clarify how a computer may help a pupil to learn. The various roles identified are considered further in Part 2.

1. A Classroom Harlequinade

Scene: A middle-ability geography class at a middle school in the Midlands

'Right, quiet everyone. Get out the maps I gave you last time and start copying down these arrows I've drawn on this big map over here. The arrows show which way the wind usually blows. I'll be back in a couple of minutes.'

The teacher dashes out, pausing only to explain to me (standing unobtrusively at the back of the classroom) that the TV has been booked by the chemistry class and that he has to fetch the small monitor which he thinks is in the labs. I have come to see a program called **Climate**[1] *in use in the classroom. Five minutes later, the teacher returns. Another five minutes later, he manages to get the micro and monitor in position and to load the program.*

'OK. Stop what you're doing for now. I want us all to have another look at this program which we played with last week. Gather round and make sure you get into a position where you can see.'

Much shuffling and moving of furniture ensues. Eventually, the teacher is able to remind the class of what the program does, which is, in essence, to present some rainfall and temperature figures as a table or a graph, to ask a series of questions, and then to seek a classification of the climate type.

'Right, look at this table and we'll see if you can answer the questions.'

The table is shown in Figure 1.1. He presses the escape key to get to the first question (Figure 1.2).

'Well, which hemisphere is it? Any ideas? Anyone?. . . Let's have another look then.'

He presses the escape key to show the table again.

'Now, is it in the northern or southern hemisphere or on the equator? Yes, Jeremy.'

'Northern.'

```
Press        For the chosen station,
 ESC
 key         Annual rainfall = 584 mm
 for         Altitude        =  25 m
question
```

```
Month      Jan   Feb   Mar   Apr   May   Jun

Rain  mm   130    81    82    57    26    16

Temp  °C     8    10    13    15    19    22


Month      Jul   Aug   Sep   Oct   Nov   Dec

Rain  mm     7     -     6    23    59    97

Temp  °C    23    21    20    17    14     9
```

Figure 1.1

'Right. How did you know that?'

'Um, because it's hotter in the summer.'

'Well, it's hotter in the summer everywhere, Jeremy. What you mean is, it's hotter in the months which are *our* summer, that is, July and August, so it's in the same hemisphere as us, that is, the northern. Is that right?'

'Yes, sir.'

With a flourish of the fingers, the teacher gets the program to ask the next question (Figure 1.3).

'OK. Now, is it cold, cool, warm or hot? What do you think? Let's look at the table again. What are the highest and lowest temperatures?'

The children at the front peer closely at the screen. The children at the back begin to chat among themselves. Some hands go up.

```
Summary
   of
answers
```

```
Which HEMISPHERE :

   1) Northern
   2) Southern
   3) On the Equator
```

```
Your choice ?
```

```
Press
 ESC
 for
table
```

Figure 1.2

'Right, Amanda, what's the lowest temperature?'

'Er, eight degrees.'

'OK, is that hot, cold, or what?'

Much discussion follows on the possible meanings of the words, hot, warm, cool and cold, in terms of normal, British day temperatures, the freezing point of water, and so on. Eventually, the children have a vote and by a majority decision decide that it's a cool climate.

'All right, we think it's cool. Let's see what the computer thinks.'

He types '2' and gets the diagram shown in Figure 1.4.

'Can anyone tell me what that means? . . . Nobody. All right, you must have all forgotten since last week.'

He then proceeds to explain that the lines give the ranges for the various temperature classifications. So, he says, anywhere where the temperature

```
┌──────────┬─────────────────────────────────────┐
│ Summary  │  In the Northern Hemisphere         │
│ of       │                                     │
│ answers  │                                     │
└──────────┴─────────────────────────────────────┘

┌──────────────────────────────────────────────────┐
│ Which THERMAL BELT :                               │
│                                                    │
│      1)   Cold                                     │
│      2)   Cool                                     │
│      3)   Warm                                     │
│      4)   Hot                                      │
│                                                    │
│                                                    │
└──────────────────────────────────────────────────┘

┌─────────────────────────────────────┐  ┌──────────┐
│                                     │  │ Press    │
│                                     │  │ ESC      │
│      Your  choice ?                 │  │ for      │
│                                     │  │ table    │
└─────────────────────────────────────┘  └──────────┘
```

Figure 1.3

lies between about −50 and +20 all year is said to be cold, and so on. (In fact, according to **Climate**, the minimum temperature has to be below −20 for a 'cold' thermal belt.) The class decide to try 'warm', and so the teacher types this in and is greeted with a screen full of nonsense and a chorus of groans from the children, who have obviously seen it all before. The computer has 'gone down'. After a few minutes, several strategic slaps, and a threat to return it to the manufacturers yet again, the computer is revived. Since **Climate** selects its tables at random, there is no way to continue with the previous example. The teacher quickly answers the first two questions for a different table to get on to the third question (Figure 1.5).

'Right, settle down. We've now got a different table and we're on

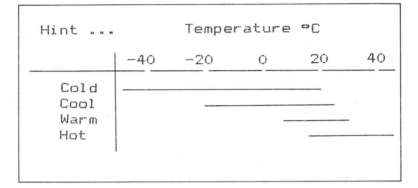

Figure 1.4

the third question: what is the latitudinal belt? Zoe, what does "latitude" mean?'

'Er, they're lines that go round the earth.'

'Show me on this map.'

Zoe waves her arm vertically.

'Well, no, that's longitude. Latitude is in this direction. The computer's asking us whether we think it is tropical, warm, cool, or arctic.'

A confused discussion then follows. This is partly because some children are still thinking about the previous 'warm' example and partly because no one seems clear of the difference between 'thermal belt' and 'latitudinal belt'. The fact that the program gives identical hints for both does not help. Even more argument is provoked when the question of rainfall distribution

```
Summary   In the Northern Hemisphere
   of     In the Cool Belt
answers
```

```
Which LATITUDINAL BELT of the globe :

   1)   Arctic
   2)   Cool Temperate
   3)   Warm Temperate
   4)   Tropical
```

```
                                           Press
                                            ESC
   Your choice ?                            for
                                           table
```

Figure 1.5

is reached (Figure 1.6). The interpretation of the hint for this proves even more difficult. Eventually, the class are satisfied by their answers to **Climate***'s five questions, and now have to classify the climate. The teacher reviews their answers so far, shown at the top of the screen (Figure 1.7).*

'OK, any ideas? Denny?'

'I can't see.'

'Well, you should have sat nearer. Come over here. Right, now, what do you think?'

Silence.

'Well, let's go through and eliminate all those which it obviously isn't. Right, is it a "hot desert"?'

The class then proceeds to eliminate all but two of the fourteen types,

```
            In the Northern Hemisphere
 Summary    In the Cool Belt
   of       In the Cool Temperate Belt
 answers    It has Moderate Rain
```

```
Comment on DISTRIBUTION of rainfall :

    1)   Rain all year
    2)   Drought all year
    3)   Summer rain,winter drought
    4)   Winter rain,summer drought
    5)   Rain all year,summer maximum
    6)   Rain all year,winter maximum
```

```
                                              Press
                                               ESC
    Your choice ?                              for
                                              table
```

Figure 1.6

leaving 'Laurentian' (because no one can remember what it is) and 'Cool Temperate Interior'. As the teacher works through the climates, he does a quick revision of what they mean; for example, he distinguishes between 'Taiga' and 'Tundra' in terms of the vegetation that grows there.

'OK, so we've only two left: Laurentian and Cool Temperate Interior. What did we say last week about the rainfall in the interior of continents?'

'There isn't very much, I think.'

'Why not?'

'There just isn't.'

'No, we can do better than that, Richard. Yes, Sue?'

'It's something to do with the clouds from the sea not reaching that far.'

Summary of answers	In the Northern Hemisphere In the Cool Belt In the Cool Temperate Belt It has Moderate Rain Summer Rain, Winter Drought

Which CLIMATE :

1) Hot Desert	8) Equatorial
2) Modified Equatorial	9) Monsoon
3) Tropical Marine	10) Savanna
4) Mediterranean	11) China
5) British Isles	12) Taiga
6) Laurentian	13) Tundra
7) Cool Temp. Interior	14) Polar

Your choice ?	Press ESC for table

Figure 1.7

'OK. So places on the coast tend to get more rain than ones inland. Now, does this place get much rain?'
'Quite a bit.'
'So, is it Cool Temperate Interior?'
'I suppose not.'
'So what must it be?'
'The other one.'
'Well, let's see.'

He types in '6' (for Laurentian), which the program says is correct, to muted cheers from the children.

'Yes, it's Laurentian, which is the name for the type of climate on the St Laurence River in Canada, which is close to the sea, as we said it should be. Now, we've only fifteen minutes left, so you can go back to your desks. You can take it in turns to use the program, you four first, and the rest of you can look at the graphs in your atlas and ask yourself the questions that the computer would ask.'

The group of four gather in front of the micro, one child monopolising the keyboard. The teacher gets them started and leaves them to answer the questions. They have no problems in using the program but their attempts at answering the questions seem little better than guesses. The teacher rejoins them. It transpires that they are confused between the rainfall and temperature entries in the graph. Eventually, the group decide that their climate is a 'hot desert'. The program says 'Incorrect: it is tundra', and the teacher consoles them with the opinion that they were right about it not having much rain but they'd forgotten about the temperature.

2. Epilogue

Scenes similar to that described in Chapter 1 are being played out in classrooms throughout the country as teachers try to make the most of the micros suddenly thrust upon them. In many ways, these lessons must be considered successful. The pupils (most of them, anyway) clearly enjoy them. Teachers too are enthusiastic and will vouch for their educational effectiveness. And yet, while watching several such lessons and looking into many more educational software products, I have become increasingly uneasy. Not only is most existing educational software of poor quality, as is generally conceded, but there are, in my opinion, deep problems with even the best programs. Worse still, this is not a passing phase, a consequence of our transitory ignorance of how to use computers effectively to aid learning.

One symptom of malaise is the general eagerness to form superficial judgements of educational software products. Another symptom is a reluctance to look for general messages from programs outside one's own specialism. While there are of course differences in the design of software suitable for four-year-olds and for forty-year-olds, there are also similarities. Most educational software products are more expensive than textbooks and they should be critically examined in the same way—only more so!, because we have not yet learned what it is reasonable to expect from educational software. Let us begin by taking a close look at the **Climate** program.

Climate presents the user with data for mean monthly temperature and rainfall and, through a series of multiple-choice questions, leads the user to a conclusion about the type of climate under consideration. According to the accompanying documentation, **Climate** may be used for both classroom demonstration and by an individual pupil.

Let us imagine a pupil using **Climate** on his own. The five multiple-choice questions which the program asks the pupil are shown in Figure 2.1, together with the possible answers for each question. If the pupil answers a question incorrectly, a graphical hint is given. After answering all five questions correctly, the pupil has to try to classify the climate as one of the fourteen types shown in Figure 1.7.

```
Questions                  Possible Answers
Which hemisphere?          northern, southern, equatorial
Which thermal belt?        cold, cool, warm, hot
Which latitudinal belt?    arctic, cool, warm, tropics
Comment on rainfall        very light, light, moderate, heavy
Comment on distribution    rain all year, drought, summer rain,
                           winter rain, summer max, winter max
```

Figure 2.1

The **Climate** program has access to data from 56 weather stations but only 28 of these are significantly different from one another. I have summarised some of these data in Figure 2.2

Our first question must be: What is the pupil expected to learn from this program? The documentation says that pupils find difficulty 'when encountering the disciplines of causality and identification for the first time. This program is designed to provide them with practice in these important disciplines.' What does this mean?

The pupil is faced with a classification task, and as in any such

```
Station    Answers to the 5 questions                    Classification
Number

1    northern, hot, tropics, very light, drought         Hot Desert
4    southern, hot, tropics, very light, drought         Hot Desert
5    equatorial, warm, tropics, heavy, rain all year     Modified Equatorial
8    northern, hot, tropics, heavy, rain all year        Tropical Marine
.             .                                                  .
.             .                                                  .
46   northern, cold, arctic, light, summer max           Taiga
49   northern, cold, arctic, very light, drought         Taiga
50   northern, cold, arctic, light, summer max           Tundra
53   northern, cold, arctic, very light, drought         Tundra
54   northern, cold, arctic, very light, drought         Polar
```

Figure 2.2

task there are several sub-tasks which have to be mastered. These
are:

1. To identify the relevant features (such as temperature, rainfall
distribution, etc.);
2. To 'evaluate' those features (for example, to work out what the
rainfall distribution is);
3. To use known rules based on these features to derive a
classification (for example, to infer that anywhere which is both
hot and dry is a 'Hot Desert');
4. To discover new rules for new situations (for example, to
induce the definition of 'Taiga' from the examples seen).

Let us consider each of these in turn. First, with **Climate** the pupil
does not have to identify the relevant features: the program asks five
questions (always the same five and always in the same order) and
there is a strong implication that all and only the five features
identified in these questions are relevant. Secondly, **Climate** does
provide practice at evaluating these features, but this is really
quite straightforward since the pupil has only to know the
(somewhat arbitrary) definitions built into the program—for
example, that 'moderate' rainfall means 500–1000 mm of rain a
year. A mistake leads the program to give a graphical representation
of this definition (always the same, regardless of which particular
mistake the pupil has made or how many). Thirdly, if **Climate** is
intended to give practice using previously learned classification
rules, then it seems odd that the program does not acknowledge
the existence of such rules. It does not, for example, give any sort
of hint or comment, other than a blunt 'incorrect', if the pupil
misclassifies the climate. Fourthly, imagine that a pupil does not
know what a Hot Desert is and is using this program to find out.
The only two stations which relate to Hot Desert are the first two
entries in Figure 2.2. So what is the rule? Does it have to be in the
tropics? Must it not be on the equator? There simply is not enough
information from which to generalise. Of course, you probably
already have a good idea about what a Hot Desert is, but what
about Laurentian and Taiga?

In short, it is not clear what the program is designed to teach. In
part, this confusion arises because the designers have not stated
their assumptions about the knowledge built into the program.

Consider, for example, the implication that all and only the five features identified in the questions are relevant. It is obvious that not all five questions have to be answered in order to derive a classification—there are 1152 (i.e. 3×4×4×4×6) possible ways to answer the five questions, but only 28 of these sequences arise. So, for example, if the answer to the fourth question is 'very light' then the fifth question need not be asked, for the answer must be 'drought'. Similarly, whatever the answer is to the second question then in 27 cases out of the 28 the answer to the third question corresponds (i.e. the answers occur in 'pairs': cold—arctic, cool—cool, warm—warm, hot—tropics).

Imagine a pupil who does not know the difference between 'thermal belt' and 'latitudinal belt': is he to conclude that they are the same thing? Even the clues that **Climate** gives after incorrect answers to these two questions are the same. The one case where these two answers differ occurs with station 5, which we can compare with station 28 (Figure 2.3). Why is station 5 considered to be in the tropics, when **Climate**'s own clue says it should be considered warm? Well, the answer is presumably that station 5 is at an altitude of 2880 m, whereas station 28 is at 49 m. I say presumably because **Climate** makes no comment on this apparently anomalous result (although, to be fair, the altitude is shown in the initial presentation of the data). But imagine a pupil who does not notice this fact—there is nothing in the questions to suggest that he should take any notice of altitude.

```
Station
Number

5    rainfall       99 112 142 125 137 143 120 130  69 112  97  79
     temperature    15  15  16  15  15  15  15  15  16  15  15  15

     equatorial, warm, tropics, heavy, rain all year --> Modified Equatorial


28   rainfall      200 196 250 230 240 230 200 225 250 220 200 205
     temperature    26  26  27  26  26  26  26  26  27  26  26  26

     equatorial, hot, tropics, heavy, rain all year --> Equatorial
```

Figure 2.3

So, the five features which **Climate** identifies are *not* sufficient to classify climates even with these artificial data (the data are not from real weather stations but 'theoretical' ones): we have found a sixth: altitude. **Climate**'s five features are not independent, and not necessary or sufficient to classify climates. In fact, it is obvious from Figure 2.2 that answering the five questions correctly still did not give the pupil sufficient information to classify the climate.

Look at stations 49, 53 and 54: exactly the same sequence of answers leads to three different classifications. Why? Altitude is not the reason this time, for all three stations are at sea level. Figure 2.4 gives the data for these three stations. A pupil unsure of

```
Station
Number


49   rainfall      2    4    0    1   11   13   20   17    8    7    8    4
     temperature  -40  -38  -32  -22  -12    4   12    8    5    0  -20  -35


   . northern, cold, arctic, very light, drought --> Taiga


53   rainfall     11   21    9   16   16   16   18   18   14    9   15   22
     temperature  -24  -20   -9   -5    3    5    8    6    4    0  -11  -17

     northern, cold, arctic, very light, drought --> Tundra


54   rainfall      0    0   10    8    0   12   13   11   20   11    0    4
     temperature  -40  -30  -20  -15   -9   -2    0   -4   -7  -17  -28  -37

     northern, cold, arctic, very light, drought --> Polar
```

Figure 2.4

the difference between Taiga, Tundra and Polar will look in vain for help from **Climate**—**Climate** will, apparently arbitrarily, label some of his classifications as 'incorrect', and that is all. A pupil may be inclined to accept such unquestionable dogmatism, but we may question whether **Climate**'s answers are themselves 'correct'.

On consulting various standard texts on climatology, I found first a classification due to Strahler.[1] He also gives fourteen climate types: Wet Equatorial, Trade Wind Littoral, Tropical Desert, West Coast Desert, Tropical Wet—Dry, Humid Subtropical, Marine West Coast, Mediterranean, Middle Latitude Desert, Humid Continental, Continental Sub-Arctic, Marine Sub-Arctic, Tundra and Icecap. Only two climate types are the same as **Climate**'s! Why should a pupil unfortunate enough to have learned Strahler's classification system be categorically told that his answers are incorrect? Moreover, Strahler's system is not the only one: there are many others, some based on quite sophisticated mathematical formulaes. Climatology is, it seems, a very complex science.

Why, we might ask (and it would be a good question for a pupil to ask), bother to classify climates at all? Climate types unlike, for example, insect types do not have precise boundaries. In one sense, all classification schemes are devised for the sake of convenience. It helps to have a word or a phrase which can be used instead of a long definition. So we use the word 'desert' expecting everyone to have at least a rough idea of what is meant. Sometimes we use such a word to avoid having to say exactly what it means. Just how dry does a desert have to be to count as a desert? A precise answer, such as 'less than 25 mm rain a year', leads naturally to the response: 'Why 25 mm and not 30 mm?'

It is in asking such why questions that we begin to see the real point of classifying climates. It is not just to give us a convenient shorthand, but to provide a system which helps us to explain and understand different climates. So, a word like 'monsoon' is useful not just as a label but because it conjures up a picture of the *cause* of the climate: a particular combination of wind, sea and temperature. We can see this explanatory role of classifications by looking at the increasingly complex schemes created by climatologists.

First of all, there are schemes based directly on vegetation. These will say, for example, that a climate is tropical if its coldest month is hot enough to allow certain (tropical) plants to grow; that is, the mean temperature of the coldest month is at least 18° C. This, then, explains one otherwise arbitrary definition used by **Climate**. Similarly, such a scheme will distinguish between Taiga and Tundra by vegetation (the former is a pine forest and the latter is treeless). But, of course, whether or not trees grow is determined partly by rainfall and temperature (it usually requires at least three months with temperatures above 6° C for trees to grow). The second kind of classification scheme is based on 'moisture budgets' and thus tries to explain vegetation. These schemes make use of formulae involving temperature, rainfall, distribution, length of day, soil, and so on. Thirdly, we have 'genetic' classifications, which seek even more explanatory power by relating climates to wind régimes and air masses. Often rainfall and temperature do not appear explicitly in such schemes: Strahler's scheme is of this kind.

Most readers will probably not be very interested in climatology, but the point is that while a good geography teacher will know all this and much more, **Climate** does not, in any significant sense, know any of it. In order to design and to judge a program like **Climate** it is necessary to know the subject-matter. We have said nothing about **Climate**'s use of graphics or its 'user-friendliness' (both of which are of a relatively high standard) because these are literally superficial: they are a gloss to cover a lack of substance. **Climate** cannot answer any of the questions which a pupil ought to ask.

Is this criticism fair and, if so, does it matter anyway? Any criticism has to be balanced against the aims and philosophies of those responsible for the product. According to the managing director of the team which developed **Climate**, the style of program is such that 'the computer is . . . neutral. It presents information but does none of the teaching.'[2] Well, the 'information' presented by **Climate** can be summarised on one A4 sheet— it is Figure 2.2, and the definition of the terms therein. If it were simply a matter of presenting information, a sheet of paper would seem perfectly adequate. In fact, since **Climate** does not use real data it scarcely presents 'information' at all. No, the merits of **Climate** lie not in the information it presents but derive precisely from the fact that the computer can contribute to teaching and, more importantly, to learning.

In what sense could one say that **Climate** 'does none of the teaching'? To answer this it is desirable, of course, to try to say what 'teaching' is. According to Hirst,[3]

a teaching activity is the activity of a person, A (the teacher), the intention of which is to bring about an activity (learning), by a person, B (the pupil), the intention of which is to achieve some end state (e.g. knowing, appreciating) whose object is X (e.g. a belief, attitude, skill).

It is not, I think, reasonable to insist that the teacher, A, be a person for an activity to qualify as teaching: it is the activity which matters, not who, or what, performs it. Presumably, the designers of **Climate** intended learning to occur to achieve some object X, even if they did not say explicitly what X would be, and so the rest of the definition seems to hold. In fact, the main reason for disqualifying **Climate** from the teaching ranks is that the activity is not one which we willingly picture a good human teacher carrying out. To see why, we need look no further than the two conditions which, according to Hirst, teaching activities must meet.

The first is that 'the activity must, either implicitly or explicitly, express or embody the X to be learnt, so that this X is clearly indicated to the pupil as what he is to learn.' **Climate** certainly does not explicitly express X, and if it is implicit it is not clear to me, for one, what it is. **Climate** makes no attempt to ensure that the pupil understands what he is to learn and does not justify, explain or demonstrate the X in any way.

The second condition is that the activity 'must take place at a level where the pupil can take on what it is intended he should learn.' **Climate** takes no steps to ensure that this is so. It does not adjust the level to suit the pupil. It will respond in exactly the same way, regardless of the pupil's ability in learning X. Of course, when **Climate** is used as a classroom demonstration (as in our scene in Chapter 1), the teacher will do what he can to ensure that these two conditions are met.

So **Climate** does not itself teach X (although one could imagine a differently programmed version of **Climate** which might be said to teach); but is it 'neutral'? An automatic washing-machine may perhaps be said to be neutral in that it doesn't make any difference what clothes are put in: they will all get swirled round and come out clean. A washing-machine, however, reflects its designer's view of the needs of its users, and there is a consensus about what these needs are. Similarly, **Climate** is neutral in that it does not matter what users type in, they all receive the same responses—and come out brainwashed (?). But **Climate**, too, reflects its designer's view of the needs of its users. In this case, however, there is little consensus. Various assumptions are built into **Climate** and to the extent that these are questionable **Climate** is not neutral. For example, **Climate** discourages pupils from asking questions (there is simply no mechanism for them to do so); it suggests that these sorts of problems can be solved by memorising a small set of questions to ask; it assumes that a successful teaching strategy is to ask short questions which must be successfully answered; it assumes that displaying information on a computer screen rather than on, say, overheads, helps pupils to learn. In other words, while **Climate** is neutral in the sense of impartial or objective, it is not neutral in terms of the affective response elicited from pupils nor in terms of its underlying educational philosophy.

One danger in concentrating on one particular program in this way is that the reader may assume that this program has been selected precisely because it has defects not shared by most educational software. Other programs may well not have **Climate**'s defects, but they will certainly have others. To be fair, **Climate** does have its virtues: it is entirely free of bugs (as far as I am aware); it is very easy to use; the layout of information on the screen is relatively clear. In fact, by present standards, **Climate** rates highly. One reviewer described it as 'indubitably excellent'.[4] Another considered that 'the program represents an intelligent and interesting approach to drill and practice [and is] good value for money.'[5] Yet a third thought that **Climate** showed that 'the standard of software to support [the microcomputer] seems to be improving dramatically.'[6] **Climate** was produced by Five Ways, one of the three major centres subsidised under the UK Government's Microelectronics Education Programme (MEP) to produce computer-assisted learning (CAL) material. The director of the MEP considers that Five Ways gives a 'quick throughput of very high quality programs'.[7]

3. The Computer as an Educational Medium

This book is about the design of educational software, that is, computer programs intended to aid learning. It is *not* about:

1. software for educational administration, such as programs for timetabling and maintaining school records, for these are standard data processing applications for which no novel techniques are necessary;
2. the content of computer studies courses at school or university;
3. educational hardware, that is, computer machinery on which educational software may be run;
4. educational philosophy, in the sense that I am not concerned to promote any particular philosophy, but with considering how software may be designed to support *any* desired philosophy;
5. the miracles of the new information technology.

I take it as read that the use of computers will be increasingly widespread, that they are capable of wonderful feats, that they will be welcomed by many teachers and pupils, and that they are bound to have a profound effect on education, both at school and at home.

My focus is on educational software as technical objects. While this software does cause us to rethink the nature of education, and computer technology does continue to develop astonishingly, it now seems possible to limit ourselves to the software itself, without a lengthy, and yet still superficial, discussion of education and computer hardware. Books exist on, for example, commercial software, legal software and medical software and their authors do not worry unduly about the nature of commerce, law and medicine. Likewise, I shall not address myself directly to the nature of education. Effective computer-aided learning depends upon the design of good educational software, so there will be enough to think about.

My main strategy will be to look critically at existing educational software. It seems to me that progress is unlikely if we allow ourselves to be overawed by what present programs can do, or if we permit ourselves to talk vaguely about even better programs which will be available 'soon'. Let us try to say clearly what we like and do not like about the programs we actually have. My criticisms are not intended to impute incompetence: they are offered in a Popperian spirit, in the hope that improvements may come about if shortcomings are actively sought out, rather than concealed or passed over. Most books about computers in education are imbued with the spirit of the exclamation mark: a more appropriate symbol for this one would be the question mark. By asking questions, I do not mean to imply that I have any answers. We are profoundly ignorant about the educational process and computers have done little to change this.

I shall begin by looking briefly at the functions of educational media in general and the computer in particular. First, what is an 'educational medium'? A spiritual medium is a person through whom spirits are said to communicate with the material world. An educational medium is a device through which absent teachers are said to communicate with pupils. For example, an Open University student may watch a televised lecture: the lecturer is not, of course, physically present, but his thoughts and ideas are, none the less, communicated to the student. We may say that the student is 'learning through the medium of television'.

But there is more to it than this. First, it is not necessary for the educational medium to stand in for the absent teacher, that is, to do whatever the teacher would do if he were present. A television programme may be of a formal lecture or of a classroom demonstration, but it may also be of some activity which no teacher could perform even if present—for example, a nuclear explosion. So educational media can be used, and are probably better used, to supplement, not replicate, functions carried out by human teachers.

Secondly, there is the question of who controls the use of the medium. No educational medium will by itself initiate anything and so someone, the absent teacher, has to design some activity to be carried out using the medium. However, the absent teacher clearly cannot control the medium. In the case of our lone Open

University student control is entirely in his hands (but in the case of televised broadcasts there are very few control options open to him). If a class of students were watching the broadcast then control would be shared among them. More often, there is a third person, in addition to the absent teacher and the pupil(s), who takes control: another teacher, who may decide, for example, to turn the sound down briefly while he elaborates some point or administers some discipline. He therefore may distort the message intended by the absent teacher who designed the activity. Some media are more clearly associated with teacher-control than television is; for example, the overhead projector. In some cases, the teacher present may use material that he has himself prepared (e.g. his own overhead transparencies). In other words, the absent teacher and the present teacher may be one and the same person.

Thirdly, we must consider the role of the designer of the educational medium itself. Media are not natural phenomena but are devices designed to perform a function. Some media seem 'intrinsically educational' in that we cannot easily see them serving any other function (e.g. the overhead projector), but more often media are coincidentally educational in that the designer has functions other than the purely educational in mind (e.g. the film projector and the computer). Consequently, the designer and the user of material with educational media must often accommodate themselves to using media not ideal for their purposes.

To sum up, then, our view of educational media is as shown in Figure 3.1. There are four classes of people involved: media designers, material designers, teachers and pupils, and control of the medium is in some way shared among them.

If a definition of the term 'educational medium' were attempted it would probably cover the following three points:

1: It is a device—a piece of hardware—through which some educational material ('software') is presented in some way;[1]
2: It provides indirect or 'mediated' experience rather than direct experience;
3: It not only represents itself but also refers to something else—so, for example, a computer studied solely as a computer would not be regarded as an educational medium.

However, looking for precise definitions will lead us nowhere,

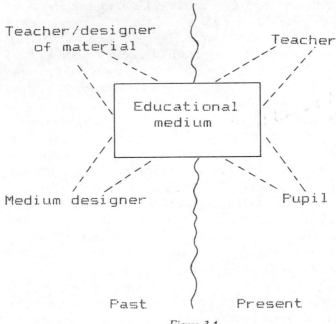

Figure 3.1

only astray. As I have said, media are functional, not phenomeno-
logical concepts, and to attempt to define them is futile. We must
concentrate on the *functions* they can perform and consider the
extent to which these functions may be educational.

So, what counts as educational? I would venture that a function
is educational simply if there is an intention that learning occurs.
The intention is held by one or more of the four individuals
identified in Figure 3.1 (but not necessarily by all). We must
therefore focus, not on the equipment or devices themselves, but
on the functions that media should be able to perform, and then
consider the extent to which a particular technology (in our case,
the computer) can support them.

An analysis of the functions of educational media may be carried
out to great detail, but Rowntree[2] gives us an appropriate
beginning. He lists six functions:

1. Engage the student's motivation.
2. Recall earlier learning.
3. Provide new learning stimuli.

Good ed practice?

4. Activate the student's response.
5. Give speedy feedback.
6. Encourage appropriate practice.

To these six functions I shall add two more:

7. Sequence learning.
8. Provide a resource.

These functions are, of course, not independent and may be going on simultaneously in any learning situation.

Now let us look briefly at each of these functions in turn.

Engaging motivation

According to Rowntree, a pupil is motivated when he identifies with the objectives to which the learning leads. Motivation may be stimulated by teachers or media (using persuasion or even bribery) but ultimately it derives from the pupil's own attitude to the particular objectives. Sometimes, because of a lack of relevant knowledge, a pupil may be unable to appreciate the objectives. In such a case, it is especially important that the objectives be explained.

The **Climate** program which we looked at in Chapters 1 and 2 does not seek to engage motivation in this sense, since it does nothing to help a pupil identify with the objectives—indeed, it does not indicate what the objectives are. Like most CAL programs, **Climate** assumes that a teacher has already done this. None the less, the first few pages of a textbook, or the first few minutes of a film or CAL program, may profitably be aimed at motivation.

Recalling earlier learning

Most learning theories assume that a pupil learns only if he has mastered certain prerequisites (by definition of 'prerequisite'). It may therefore help the pupil to remind him of what he has already learned that is relevant to the new learning situation. Most educational software makes no attempt to fulfil this function, it being left to any accompanying notes or to a teacher. I shall, therefore, not consider this function further.

Providing new stimuli

Under this heading, we would include those media actions which are intended to stimulate, guide or direct the pupil towards achieving the learning objectives; for example, actions designed to focus a pupil's attention on what is thought important, or to provide variety in the presentation of ideas, or to give illustrative examples. This is probably **Climate**'s main function, for the program does, through direct questioning, focus a pupil's attention and also provides an appealing alternative to the more conventional textbook treatment of climates.

Activating pupil-responses

Educational theorists agree that meaningful learning cannot be achieved through the passive reception of knowledge, but requires active involvement on the pupil's part. This, of course, means a mental rather than physical activity. In textbooks this might be provoked by in-text questions which serve as a (rather poor) substitute for the challenging nature of a good one-to-one tutorial.

The design of many CAL programs reflects an inadequate view of what is meant by an 'active response'. Often this degenerates to blind button-pressing. **Climate**, in fact, is guilty here, for pupils often resort to simply pressing all the keys in turn until they reach the 'required' one, giving no thought to the question asked at all. But CAL is not alone in this fault. In an Edinburgh museum there is an impressive set of models of nineteenth-century industrial machinery. These models can be made to work by pressing buttons on the front of the displays. Children are inclined to run from model to model, pressing buttons as fast as possible, without stopping to see what happens.

Giving information

Rowntree emphasised the role of speedy feedback: 'knowledge of results is the life-blood of learning and it must keep flowing.' This leads on to a consideration of the nature of feedback, which may range from a blunt 'incorrect' to a sympathetic smile preceding a discussion of an alternative line of thinking. In the latter case, feedback merges into fresh teaching. Computer programs like

Climate are generally good at providing speedy feedback of the former kind. But evidence[3] and common sense suggest that feedback which provokes the pupil to an active reconsideration of what he has just said or done is more effective.

To give feedback is to provide the pupil with information he is thought to need. The information provided is to a greater or lesser extent implied by the pupil's previous responses. As we shall see, computers may be programmed to retrieve relevant information in a more flexible manner than other media. In fact, it is possible to provide ways for pupils explicitly to request information from a computer (instead of providing it only when it is thought to be needed). This is a crucial distinction: for the first time, there is a suggestion that a pupil is not dictated to by the machine (he is not 'responding to stimuli' in any straightforward way) but he is asking for information for his own means. Of course, this is only possible with media capable of sustaining an interaction of this kind.

Encouraging practice

For some skills only practice makes perfect. For example, motor skills, such as typing, must be practised as it is more a matter of polishing technique than seeking understanding. With cognitive skills, repetitive drills can only consolidate previous understanding, unless they give explanations as well as answers: 'No, the climate is Hot Desert *because*. . . .' When we consider computer drills later it will be necessary to think about the kinds of skill for which explanations can be generated. Two further (and conflicting) requirements for successful drills are that they should present problems at an appropriate level of difficulty and that the pupil should be aware of his progress towards the objectives.

Sequencing learning

With older media, such as television and textbooks, the sequence of learning activities is determined in advance by the teacher/designer, or extemporaneously by a teacher or pupil. The medium itself does not decide the learning sequence. With computers, however, it can make sense to talk of autonomous decisions to do with sequencing learning. While the slogan 'computers only do what they are programmed to do' is true in a literal sense, it is untrue in practice: programs often make decisions which surprise their programmers, and users of programs often behave as though the computer is capable of independent decision-making. The sequencing may range from a decision to move on to a more difficult class of problem in an arithmetic drill to one to change the topic of discussion in a computer-based tutorial. It is straining credulity to describe **Climate** as making autonomous decisions, for it is clearly following an entirely predetermined sequence of actions, but we shall see other programs where the responsibility is less clearly assigned.

Providing a resource

So far, the word 'medium' has dictated my interpretation of it: I have concentrated on intermediary roles. For older media this is natural, for few seriously argue that pupils should be encouraged to write overheads or develop television films for the educational benefits that would accrue (but see Maddison,[4] p. 96). However, many educationalists do believe that pupils should write computer programs, not just to learn about computer programming, but to help them learn other subjects and to help them develop general problem-solving skills. In this case, the computer serves less as a medium and more as a resource; there is less emphasis on the pre-design of learning activities and more emphasis on a pupil's self-directed activities.

These then are some of the main functions which educational media can perform. Before looking at some computer programs which illustrate these functions let us briefly summarise the capabilities of computers which might be useful. This may look like a litany of undoubted virtues, so I shall add a note of qualification as well.

First, computers are fast. They can perform numerical calculations and look up information in a database much faster than humans can and so, of course, may be used to relieve pupils of the drudgery of these tasks. But they are not fast at everything. Computers are not as fast as us in, for example, identifying faces in photographs. For many things we might like computers to do—for example, converse with us in English—the speed of computer-response depends very much on the sophistication of programming.

Secondly, computers can generate audio and visual effects. However, compared to television, computer graphics can be dull. Good graphics and sound are very expensive to produce. In addition, these audio-visual effects are easily misused, for example, to blow raspberries for incorrect answers and to play fanfares for correct ones.[5] Computer graphics and sound are more effective when combined with the computer's other capabilities.

Thirdly, computers are cheap, small and reliable. Everything is relative, of course, and in this case computers using micro-electronics are cheaper, smaller and more reliable than those of ten years ago. However, since you get what you pay for, by and large, and educational budgets are small, school micros are bound to be relatively limited in the kinds of program which can be written for them.

Fourthly, computers are interactive, that is, they can be programmed to react sensibly to what a user inputs. While computer programs are clearly more interactive than, say, television programmes, there are always limits on the kinds of thing a user can input and receive a sensible response to. Often the user does not know what these limits are. And the style of interaction is different from that between humans: computer output tends to be authoritative, objective, repetitive, without humour, flashy, overbearing, smarmily friendly and pretentiously knowledgeable. Though it is silly to attribute these qualities to computers, we do.

Fifthly, computers can process symbols. This gets to the essence of what kind of machine a computer is. Computers can, in principle, store and manipulate symbols representing any kind of knowledge. If a pupil types 'Hot Desert' and the computer replies 'No, it is Laurentian' then it is natural to assume that the computer actually knows what 'Laurentian' means. In reality, it is probably replying after comparing bit patterns representing the letters of 'Hot Desert' with bit patterns representing those of 'Laurentian'. The odds are that it could no more answer 'What is Laurentian?' than you or I could. Now, computers *can* be programmed to answer such questions meaningfully but it is difficult to do so. And we need to be especially careful with programs which purport to understand subjects like paranoia or political popularity (as some do) and even matters of emotion and aesthetics. Users of apparently knowledgeable programs sometimes scarcely appreciate that they are skating on a thin sliver of ice over a deep and wide pond.

Sixthly, computer programs are modifiable. Whereas a film or a textbook comes in a take-it-or-leave-it form, there is a third option (again, in principle) for a computer program: change it. Teachers are more likely to adopt that which they can adapt. However, there are few programs available today which can be modified in any significant way by the average teacher.

In Part 2 we shall look at a variety of computer programs which attempt to apply these capabilities to perform the media functions identified above. But first a few more words of caution. There are bound to be some pupils (and teachers) who react against sterile computer activities and who prefer human interaction. Even those pupils who seem highly motivated by computer activities may be badly served by being consigned to long hours at the keyboard. It is possible, for example, that their enthusiasm derives from social integration problems, which may be exacerbated by computer activities carried out in isolation. If a pupil prefers using a computer to reading a book or playing football, the proper response may be to find out why he does not like reading books or playing football, not to assign him yet more computer activities. Computer programs with apparently straightforward cognitive objectives (such as to practise multiplication skills) may carry other less obvious and less desirable messages, for example, about the way to set about learning in general, or about the way computers have to be used outside school.

PART 2
Educational Software in Action

In Part 2 we shall consider various types of educational software to try to clarify how the computer may fulfil the seven functions of educational media identified in Chapter 3. Since learning is a highly complex process, successful educational software will often owe its success to the way different functions are combined. We, however, shall look at the functions one by one.

4.   Engaging Motivation

Let us begin our search for educational software which motivates pupils by looking at some programs which do succeed in engaging the attention of users for hours with no tangible reward.

In **Adventure** games, the player typically has to locate some treasure by moving through a hazardous fantasy world. One version, called **Lost Dutchman's Gold**,[1] is set in the Superstition Mountains of Arizona and the player accompanies the ghost of a prospector who knows the secret of a gold mine. Descriptions of the player's location are shown on the screen (as in Figure 4.1) and

```
You are in a small camp.   You see :
Carrysacks. Untied burdenbeast. Leather piece. Campfire.

Obvious exits are : West North South East
=================================================================

         What do you want to do now? Get burdenbeast
? You have not the strength to do that, Sir Knight.
         What do you want to do now? Examine campfire
There's somethin' here !!
         What do you want to do now? Examine burdenbeast
You see a flop-eared ill tempered quadrapedal animal.
         What do you want to do now? Drop carrysacks
OK
```

(The two-word replies are the player's commands; the rest is output from the program.)

Figure 4.1

the player moves through the fantasy world by typing commands—usually restricted to two words, such as 'go north' or 'light match'. There is no doubting the compulsive hold that such games have over some players: each game is 'a verbal tapestry of interwoven phrases that whisk you away to magical kingdoms of the mind.'[2]

But of what relevance are games like **Adventure** to education? Some teachers apparently are enthusiastic about **Adventure** itself. Chandler[3] considers that 'the usefulness of the program genre of

Adventure games has now been widely recognised.' Mullan[4] comments on their 'terrific motivational aspect.' Another reviewer thought that **Adventure** games were 'important and valuable resources for learning'.[5] Chandler lists the following merits of **Adventure**:

1. It encourages precision with language;
2. it encourages cooperation and group discussion and decision-making;
3. it develops oral skills;
4. it demands thinking logically and laterally; and
5. it develops screen-reading technique, familiarity with the keyboard, etc.

Of course, children have to practise reading skills to play the game, but the sentences displayed are usually poor samples of English literature (often featuring spelling mistakes, as in Figure 4.1), and it is hard to believe that a restriction to two-word imperatives is conducive to the development of good communication skills. What kind of a model of language use is a program which spouts words (like 'campfire' and 'ill tempered') with no notion of their meaning at all?

Adventure games are commercially produced for home entertainment. There are difficult organisational questions to be solved if they are to be useful in the classroom. Generally, a group of children will play the game together, rationalised as an attempt to encourage cooperation rather than competition but more often dictated by a shortage of computers. Ideally, the teacher will not be involved or will become just another member of the group but, in practice, young children cannot cope unaided with most **Adventure** games, which are intended for older players.

The continuing dearth of good educational software forces imaginative teachers to think of ways of using other available software, such as **Adventure** games, in their classes. Does this mean that **Adventure** games should count as educational software? If so, we must be prepared, for example, to count Spielberg's 'ET' as an educational film if a teacher thinks of asking his six-year-olds to write a synopsis of its plot. It would be a sad admission that we knew little about educational software design if we came to rely on the serendipitous adoption of commercial games and the like. However, the key features of **Adventure**, which seem to be fantasy, interaction and an alluring goal, can be adopted for software designed for education (as we shall see). It is interesting, incidentally, that the appeal of **Adventure** owes little to the much-vaunted computer graphics for most versions of the game use none at all, it being up to the user to supply the necessary graphic imagery. Inevitably, however, the use of graphics has proved irresistible. For example, **The Hobbit**[6] has brought 'Adventure games to a new dawn . . . [offering] a unique presentation of a classic piece of literature.'[7]

Levin and Kareev[8] chide disbelievers for thinking that computer games 'will only be a distractive and destructive force for the normal process of education'. They feel that games like **Roadrace** have 'intrinsic educational value'. **Roadrace** is a game in which a player drives a simulated car on a racetrack. The car is controlled by two paddles, one for steering, the other for acceleration. The winding racetrack scrolls down the screen as the car moves. The player's score, which is given by the distance travelled, is shown at the bottom of the screen. The game is thus like many to be found in seaside arcades. Where is its educational value? Levin and Kareev develop the following catalogue:

1. It teaches hand–eye coordination;
2. the player learns to integrate two separate streams of information;
3. it gives practice in naming numbers;
4. it could easily be modified to give practice with decimals and fractions;
5. it may help increase the span of attention of players;
6. it provides an opportunity for mastery, especially important for low-achievers;
7. it helps children learn to cooperate, especially if two take a paddle each;
8. the scores can be used to introduce maths activities such as scaling, averages, graphs, and statistics.

Levin and Kareev conclude that **Roadrace** and 'other, equally "useless" activities . . . can enhance education in the broadest sense.'

Well, maybe. But I would be happier to accept the simple

argument that games such as **Adventure**, **Roadrace**, **Space Invaders**, and so on, should be acknowledged in schools as they are now part of our culture.

Profound justifications often seem perverse: why encourage group cooperation through games based on group extermination (**Space Invaders**), cooperation not competition through a simulation of one of the most competitive sports (**Roadrace**), and the development of linguistic skills through illiterate programs (**Adventure**)? Games may certainly be used in primary schools as a first stage in computer literacy, to provide a familiarity with the keyboard, but most were never designed for this age-group. It would be miraculously convenient if commercially-produced entertainments proved to be ideal for multifarious educational purposes.

Most children enjoy computer games (and paddling in the sea) but this does not mean that the games 'engage motivation', as most commentators seem to assume. In Chapter 3, we said 'a pupil is motivated when he identifies with the objectives to which the learning leads.' Computer games are alluring, involving, even addictive but they are not necessarily motivating. The players of computer games do not have learning objectives. Ask an **Adventure** player what his objective is and he will say 'to find the treasure' not 'to improve my reading skills'. Does it matter, as long as the pupil learns even if he does not have the objectives which a teacher may like to imagine? Maybe not, if we are happy to teach by deception, that is, by introducing activities whose motive is something other than that appreciated by the pupil.

5.   Providing New Stimuli

Since most educational media can perform most of the functions listed in Chapter 3, one reason for using a computer rather than some other medium is simply to add variety. Some educational software designers seem to begin by looking at activities that have previously been carried out without computers and then try to mimic them with a computer program. Sometimes the effect is to emphasise important, but previously neglected, aspects of a particular activity.

A simple example is **Hunt the Thimble**,[1] a computer version of the well-known party game. Players specify where they wish to search and are given clues, such as 'you are getting warmer', as they proceed. The aim of the program is to develop skills with the keyboard, with reading, and with one-step decision-making. The first two we have met before: perhaps we should concede that any program which requires the use of a keyboard and a screen (i.e. all present educational software) develops these skills! As regards decision-making, the hope is that by playing the game in the abstract, without the boring digression of actually moving about and looking for a thimble, children will be able to concentrate on the logical aspects of the game. **Hunt the Thimble** is, in fact, a rather homely version of the **Adventure** game, with which it shares an aversion to the use of graphics.

Computer programs which pretend to play some role, or which encourage players to pretend to play some role, are among the most difficult to assess. Their appeal lies in their blurring reality with fantasy. We are led to the question 'What is reality?' But before getting into this, I shall briefly mention a few more programs of this kind.

Saqqara[2] is a program which simulates an actual archaeological site in Egypt: it is somewhat like an **Adventure** in which all the objects encountered are real (or rather were real in Ancient Egypt). However, as the authors of the program point out, 'archaeology is not "treasure hunting". It is a systematic, methodical enterprise requiring record keeping and mathematical exactitude.'[3] In this spirit, the program can be used as the basis for a whole term's project on Ancient Egypt, in which the work undertaken away from the computer is by far the most important aspect. Similar programs are **Inkosi**,[4] with which the player assumes the role of an African ruler deciding how much maize to sow, how many cows to kill, and so on; **Tourism**,[5] where the player has to plan the development of a tourist industry on a mythical island and then run his planned enterprise; and **Mary Rose**,[6] which simulates the raising of the galleon of that name from the seabed off the south coast of England in 1982.

Most of these programs are intended for the primary age-group—**Hunt the Thimble**, particularly, is for younger children. Now let's look at some simulations designed for secondary schoolchildren.

Simulations are being increasingly used in Computer Studies courses. This needs careful thinking about. In the 'real world', data processing programs are written to solve 'real problems': for a newsagent, to help him run his corner shop; for a supermarket, to help with stock management; for a hospital, to maintain medical records. These programs, however, cannot be used in schools because they are too expensive and often too large for school micros. Also, if we need an academic reason, the programs are too complicated for pupils to understand. So, instead, quasi-data processing programs, which pretend to solve real problems but in fact could never be used to do so, are provided: computer programs pretending to be other computer programs! Examples of such programs are **Newsagent**, **DVLC**[7] and a series of packages developed at the University of Manchester Institute of Science and Technology. The aim of these packages is to make the best use of limited computer facilities, yet retain the real-life flavour of the applications systems.[8]

In other subjects, especially the sciences, there are now a number of simulations available. An example is **Newton**,[9] a computer program which calculates the path of a satellite injected into orbit horizontally. The program is distributed with a set of

'eaflets, to form a 'unit', the objectives of which are worth quoting
n full:

1. extending students' knowledge of projectile motion from the
    simplest case (a 'flat earth' and constant gravitational force), to
    the more general (round earth, force varying with distance);
2. an appreciation of how the application of Newton's second
    law, and his law of gravitation leads to the prediction of
    satellite orbits;
3. knowledge of the possible shape of orbits;
4. some idea of the periodic time of orbits, and the effect on the
    orbit of varying injection velocity;
5. the application of a familiar idea (conservation of energy) in a
    new situation.

And more generally:

6. thinking about the relationship between a simplified model and
    the actual situation it is used to describe;
7. an appreciation of the use of a computer to solve a problem
    which students cannot solve analytically.'

To help achieve this impressive set of objectives, we would
certainly expect a powerful program to be necessary.

A pupil running **Newton** must specify the height of injection of
the satellite, its speed at injection, and the time-interval between
successive positions shown on the screen. The program will then
plot the positions traced by the simulated satellite (Figure 5.1). The
pupil may then change one or more of these three values and obtain
a second plot, and so on. Alternatively, he may ask for a table of
numerical values of the satellite's height above the earth's surface,
its speed, and the angle it has travelled since injection. And that is
all the program does.

Which of the computer's capabilities are being used here to help
achieve the objectives stated? Some possible answers are:

1. The computer's speed at calculation is being used to relieve the
    pupil of this task: indeed, the pupil is probably unable to do the
    calculation, since he does not know the relevant formulae.
2. Computer graphics are being used to attract interest, although
    there are some problems with this (the plot is too slow,
    sometimes dots from previous plots are left on the screen, and

```
Height at injection    = 500000 metres
Speed at injection     = 8000 metres/sec
Time step for output   = 100 seconds
```

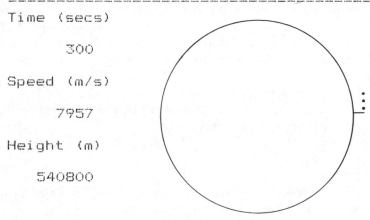

```
Time (secs)

    300

Speed (m/s)

    7957

Height (m)

  540800
```

Figure 5.1

the resolution, i.e. the precision of the drawing, on most micros is inadequate—sometimes the satellite's path appears to pass below the earth's surface!).

3. The computer simulation is an 'experiment' much more conveniently carried out than the corresponding real one, which, of course, in practice never would be. So, like many simulations, **Newton** provides vicarious experience of stimuli unobtainable in real life.

4. The 'set values and then plot' iteration provides an interaction which, if directed toward some goal, such as finding the time for a satellite to orbit once round the earth close to the surface, can sustain pupil interest.

5. The program provides a model which pupils may themselves change to see the effect: this is a possibility suggested in the last section of the accompanying teacher's notes.

Before considering the last point further, we must look briefly at how the program works as it stands. (Non-mathematicians prepared to trust that **Newton** is based upon a precise formula may skim this paragraph.) If a satellite is at position x,y (see Figure 5.2) and moving with speed v_x in the x direction and speed v_y in

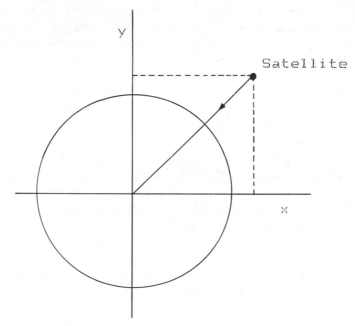

Figure 5.2

the y direction, then it can be shown that position x_t of the satellite after a small time, t, is given by:

$$x_t = x + v_x t \times k + t^2/r^3 \qquad 5.1$$

where k is a constant and $r^2 = x^2 + y^2$. Similarly, we could work out y_t and the speeds in the x and y directions after time t. So, since the initial positions and speeds are known, we can proceed to calculate the positions after successive small intervals of time. Equation 5.1 can be rewritten to form part of a computer program, as follows:

```
repeat
    r := sqrt(x*x + y*y);
    newx := x + speedx*t + k*x*t*t/(r*r*r);
    newy := y + speedy*t + k*y*t*t/(r*r*r);
    plot(newx,newy);
    recalculate(speedx,speedy);
    x := newx;  y := newy
until pupil has seen enough
```

Equation 5.1 has been derived assuming that the gravitational force obeys an inverse square law (i.e. the force is proportional to

$1/(r \times r)$ where r is the distance of the satellite from the centre of the earth). In the notes accompanying **Newton**, the first question raised in the section discussing modifications to the program is, 'What would the orbits look like if the gravitational force did not follow an inverse square law, but varied in some other way with distance?' For a pupil to investigate this, he would need to get inside the **Newton** program, find the piece of program corresponding to the fragment above, and change it in the required way. For example, if the pupil wanted to see what would happen if the gravitational force were proportional to $1/r$ then he would have to change the $(r \times r \times r)$s that occur in the above piece of program to $(r \times r)$s. (This is quite easily seen from the derivation of equation 5.1). Needless to say, for this to be possible the pupil must be able to read, understand and change the program. As we shall see in later chapters, the programmer can do a great deal to help the pupil (or teacher) to modify programs.

It is necessary now to make some general points about models and simulations. According to the dictionary, a model is 'a simplified description of a system etc. to assist calculations and predictions.' So, equation 5.1 is a simplified description of the satellite's orbit, simplified in this case in that, for example, the affect of air resistance is ignored. A computer simulation involves the use of a model to study how a system changes over time. Possible advantages of computer simulations are that they may reduce cost, time and danger, highlight what is important educationally, and enable otherwise impractical investigations to be carried out. The word 'modelling' is best reserved for an activity in which the pupil looks into the structure of the model itself, rather than observes its performance. Modifying or building models is likely to give insights into the system modelled, and of the nature and limitations of models in science, economics and other subjects, but it requires some skill to design environments in which pupils can create non-trivial models expressed as computer programs.

Computer simulations present a particularly complex form of mediated learning, the problems of which have been discussed by Bruner and Olson.[10] There is clearly a world of difference in a pupil using a simulation of, say, an expedition to Saqqara and in a pupil directly experiencing such an expedition, and it is simplistic

in the extreme to assume that the pupil learns the same sorts of
thing from both activities. Unfortunately, almost nothing is known
about just what pupils do learn from such simulations.

One problem, of course, is that all simulations are simplifications. They are idealisations intended to emphasise what is
essential to understanding a particular aspect of the system
simulated. **Newton**, for example, ignores air resistance; it assumes
that the mass of the satellite is much less than that of the earth; it
assumes that the effect of other planets is negligible, and so on. We
might not be too worried about these simplifications for we know
that scientific models are often developed with simplifying
assumptions, and in any case no such theory should ever be
considered perfect. But what about a simulation in a subject like
economics? How can we be sure that a pupil appreciates that there
are questionable simplifications built into the program? How can
we find out what these simplifications are? How can we find out
what the model actually is that the program is based on?

If a simulation is to 'emphasise what is essential to understanding'
then the designer should know what it is that is to be understood.
With **Newton**, for example, a pupil may vary the satellite's height
and speed of injection, but not its mass, although this too influences
the satellite's path. Presumably, an understanding of the effect of
mass on orbital paths is not one of the objectives of **Newton**.
However, if the aim were to investigate the impact of a satellite
crashing to earth then it would be essential to allow the value of its
mass to be varied.

Imagine now that you were designing a simulation of the role of
the prime minister of Great Britain (for such a program actually
exists, called **GB Ltd**[11]). What values would you consider it
essential for a pupil to be able to vary? First, you have to say what
the pupil is to learn. What model would the program be based on?
Would there be anything corresponding to equation 5.1 for
Newton? If not, what sort of model would it be? What sort of
models could programs like **Inkosi** and **Tourism** (mentioned
earlier) be based upon? The act of deciding what to put in such
simulations is a cultural judgement, which, once made, usually
becomes hidden in the programs and thus unquestionable.

Users of simulations do, of course, appreciate, to some extent,
that the underlying model is a simplification and they tend to

assume that the designers have a purpose in including and
excluding the features they have. Moreover, they may assume that
what is included is, in fact, essential. So, users of **Climate** may
assume that the five features which the program asks questions
about are the only ones that matter in classifying climates. If **GB
Ltd** deals wih electoral reform and the banning of fox hunting,
say, then a pupil may conclude that a consideration of these issues
is crucial to governing the country. Even worse, the results of
running a simulation may encourage quite unwarranted inferences
about the system modelled. If a pupil finds, using **GB Ltd**, that his
government is never re-elected if unemployment exceeds 10 per
cent, what is he expected to infer? How could a teacher, knowing
nothing about the model programmed, comment sensibly on this?

Finally, in this section let us look at a simulation which neatly
encapsulates many of the problems with this kind of educational
software. **Litter**[12] is a program distribued to all UK primary
schools which participate in the government's Micros in Schools
scheme. With **Litter**, a pupil plays the role of a local councillor
who is seeking re-election and decides to run an anti-litter
campaign. The councillor has £1500 to spend and for each of ten
weeks has to decide upon a strategy to reduce the amount of litter
on the streets (without over-spending) and to secure the
popularity of the voters. Figure 5.3 shows a typical screen display
from **Litter**. The column on the left shows the councillor's
popularity. The box in the middle gives the options (send out the
police daily, put up posters, provide extra bins, deliver leaflets,
employ extra cleaners, advertise on television). After selecting
one or more of these options, the money remaining and the
councillor's popularity are adjusted accordingly.

Again, we must ask what the objectives are. According to the
documentation, **Litter** 'will enable users to:

— formulate strategies and make decisions relating to local
council elections by engaging in purposeful discussion;

— be aware of the results of their decisions by using a
microcomputer simulation;

— practise their arithmetic skills by planning financial
expenditure.'

The third we may concede, for this is an incidental objective.
The main point is that the designers believe that **Litter** helps to

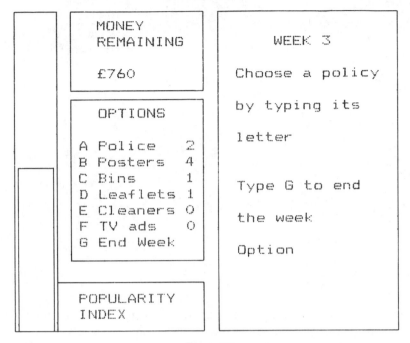

Figure 5.3

develop decision-making skills. This is a different sort of objective from those behind the design of **Newton** and similar simulations. With **Newton**, a pupil is expected to learn some physics, not by discovering equation 5.1—that would be too optimistic—but by developing intuitions about how changing the variables affects what happens. With **Litter**, a pupil is expected to make decisions, but he is not expected to learn any politics—or is he? How is it possible to 'formulate strategies and make decisions' and judge your success without a meaningful context? **Litter** certainly enables pupils to make decisions, but unless it is possible to relate these decisions to what happens both in the simulated world and the real world the exercise is literally a meaningless game.

So how are decisions related to what happens in **Litter**'s simulated world? Or, in other words, what is the model upon which **Litter** is based? Is there anything like **Newton**'s equation 5.1? Figure 5.4 indicates how **Litter** works. For each policy option, and for each week, there are values indicating the cost, litter

Policy	Week	Cost	Litter collected (Kg)	Popularity rating (%)
Police				
	1	150	1800	10
	2	100	2010	18
	3	50	2100	25
	4	0	1980	29
	5	-50	1800	30
	6	-50	1710	27
	7	-50	1610	15
	8	-15	1590	-3
	9	-25	1530	-10
	10	-25	1500	-21

Figure 5.4

collected and the effect on popularity. As you can see, the values appear arbitrary—why does the cost of sending the police out vary from week to week (and do the police actually pay some weeks!)? The values seem to be mere creations of the imagination. It would be possible to write a version of **Newton** which used tables of numbers (such as Kepler's experimental observations now made redundant by Isaac Newton's mathematical formalisation). The objection to **Litter**'s numbers is not that they are numbers but that they bear no relation to reality—the values are not experimental observations! Of course, we should have known this all along. How could a computer program make sensible judgements about political popularity when we know virtually nothing about it ourselves? How easy it is to believe that a computer always knows what it is doing just because it can do some things very well. (Did *you* question the 'accordingly' that crept in at the end of the last paragraph but one?) The designers of **Litter** have the effrontery to suggest that, after using **Litter**, the following questions might be asked: 'Would this program help a real-life councillor to plan his campaign? Would he be wise to rely on it totally for his decisions?'

6.   Activating Pupil-Response

It is accepted by all (except advocates of learning while sleeping or under hypnosis) that a pupil must take an active part in the proceedings, seeing them as relevant and important to him. How can computers help ensure pupils are actively involved?

First it is necessary to clarify what is meant by 'active'. Apart from programs designed to teach typing or to help pupils learn basic motor skills, all educational software is concerned with the development of intellectual abilities, so we must look for programs which stimulate thought not movement, be it only of the finger. Many programs, such as computer games, will do nothing unless constantly prodded by the user, but this does not necessarily mean that the user is actively involved in our sense.

Consider first the **Drake** program,[1] which, like some of those mentioned in Chapter 5, is a role-playing simulation. The program describes events during Sir Francis Drake's voyage round the world in 1577 (see Figure 6.1). Every so often the pupil has to make

```
Plot/Log    Depart Cape Horn 30th Oct.
            Sail north. Supplies running low.
            Search various islands for food. No luck.
            Eventually encounter an Indian. (N/M7).
            He indicates that he can take you to
            a place where there is food.

Decision 4    Do you A) trust him and follow (he might
                         lead you into a trap.)
                      B) kill the Indian and continue
                         your search.
Type A or B
A
Bold move. This is what Drake did. The Indian directed him
to Valparaiso (Plot M7) and he took stores
wine and cedarwood from this small settlement. He was
in luck. The treasure ship 'The Grand Captain of the Sea'
was anchored there. He took 400lb of gold from it.
```

Figure 6.1

a decision about a problem that has arisen, which is presented as a multiple-choice question. When the pupil has answered, the program comments on his decision. The program is intended to develop decision-making skills as well as teach some history. The aim then is to make the pupil reach decisions while the program is running, rather than to set values once, and then sit back and watch. It takes only a slight change in emphasis to turn a program like **Drake** into a computerised version of a programmed textbook.

In its simplest form, a programmed book presents on each page a question and some possible answers, with associated page numbers. The reader has to turn to the page indicated for the answer he considers correct. An example from a computerised version is given in Figure 6.2, which shows two frames from a program called **World War One**.[2] Such programs are often called 'branching programs'. This mechanistic style has a relatively long tradition in computer-assisted learning. The first such programs, derived from the operant conditioning theories underlying the then fashionable 'teaching machines', were written in the early 1960s. Re-reading the early literature induces a strong feeling of *plus ça change*:

programmed instruction is in part a response to the challenge of providing for individual differences among learners. Should large numbers of good programs ever become available—and the lack of them and the difficulty of writing good ones together, currently, constitute a formidable bottleneck—students will be able to work successfully and competently by themselves . . . Programmed teaching machines, in turn linked to computers, may prove to be useful tools in fashioning more productive theoretical formulations.[3]

Today, such branching programs are most commonly found in computer-based training schemes, since adult employees are more likely to accept the rigidity of this teaching approach. In fact, there are many reasons why computer-based training, however it is implemented, is becoming increasingly attractive. By providing courses which can be taken by students at a time and place that suits them, the substantial travel and accommodation costs associated with bringing students together for residential courses are eliminated. Such courses are particularly suitable for updating computer salesmen, for example, where access to equipment is not a problem.

Thus by 1907 Europe was divided into
two sets of countries.

The Triple Alliance dating from 1882
was composed of Germany, Austria-
Hungary and Italy.

The Triple Entente dating from 1907
was composed of France, Russia and
Britain.

The first was a military alliance, the
second a much looser agreement with no
military commitments upon the members at
the start.

Are the details of this frame correct?

      A.   Yes
      B.   No

PRESS THE KEY OF YOUR CHOICE

In fact the previous frame was correct!

If you do not feel you know the
alliances well enough then perhaps you
should go back to the start of this
section.

However, you may wish to carry on.

      A.   Back to start
      B.   Next frame

PRESS THE KEY OF YOUR CHOICE

Figure 6.2

Outside industrial and commercial training courses, however, branching programs have been largely rejected: pupils find them boring, and teachers find them time-consuming to produce. They seem especially unsuitable for younger pupils. About the only kind of pupil likely to accept them is the highly coerced or the desperate, e.g. worried imminent examinees. Recently Smith,[4] while lamenting 'the need for good educational programs which are well-thought-out', has described a series of such programs for O level biology revision.

But, there must be more subtle ways of encouraging pupil involvement than bombarding him with questions. Let us go to the other extreme and consider the **Snooker**[5] program that asks no questions but just presents a challenge, a picture of a snooker table with a ball on it. There are no instructions, and the user attracted by the bait of trying to pot the ball has to work out for himself how to do so. Fundamentally, of course, the program is a drill on angle estimation, but to children it's just a challenging game. The appeal of the game derives crucially from the fact that there is no need for the program to label each estimate as right or wrong—it is sufficient to see where the ball moves across the table. Notice that this program is *not* a snooker simulation: the role of the snooker table is simply to provide an appealing context.

Most computer games activate responses, as **Snooker** does, by presenting an irresistible challenge. With simulations, the challenge has often to be created outside the program, for example, 'find the shape of an orbit'. So far, most of the programs discussed have been designed to be used by the pupil or group of pupils without a teacher present. In these cases, it is essential for the programs themselves to sustain interest. But if a teacher is present a new set of solutions (and problems) becomes possible. The shortage of school micros and the difficulty of designing stand-alone programs are sufficient reasons for looking at programs designed to be used by a teacher as 'electronic blackboards'. Organisationally, such programs have a role in schools which have enough computers for one to be routinely available to teachers (like ordinary blackboards) but not enough computers for one to be routinely available to pupils.

Any program could be used as a classroom demonstration but for this to be successful the program should:

1. add to what a teacher could do unaided;
2. be easily adapted by the teacher to suit his own teaching style;
3. be easily usable by the teacher;
4. stimulate and involve the class even though technical control remains with the teacher.

Since a computer can only do what it has been programmed to do, and since teachers cannot be expected to modify programs during a lesson, it follows that 'electronic backboard' programs should be carefully designed and tested in classrooms to anticipate the teacher's requirements and to provide him with a flexible set of options.

Barset[6] is an example of such a program. Here, the program can, under teacher control, be made to display pictures of animals in various arrangements: randomly, in groups, as bar charts, and so on. The idea is to get pupils to think about the different ways in which information can be presented and to introduce some basic mathematical ideas. Now, there is no sensible way in which this program can be used directly by children: it is designed to be used as a teacher's assistant. The particular virtues of the computer exploited are: its speed and accuracy, its ability to produce an unlimited variety of drawings, and to move easily from one form of presentation to another. Likewise, the program tries to capitalise on the teacher's virtues: his ability to produce questions and explanations extemporaneously and to deal sympathetically with any problems that arise.

To use **Barset** successfully, a teacher must be very familiar with what the program can do and must carefully plan a lesson of a somewhat didactic style. There are other kinds of electronic blackboard programs where the teacher is placed more on the side of the pupils. Perhaps an **Adventure** game could be considered in this way, if the teacher guides the activity without himself knowing the solution. A classic in this style, however, is the **Janeplus** program,[7] in which the class has to guess the functional relationship between two numbers after seeing example pairings. The teacher's role is to control the class discussion and perhaps to type in the class's suggestions. Some educationalists emphasise the way in which such programs may help to break down the pupil's perception of the teacher as the source of authority and knowledge (although some teachers may not be so keen!).

On the other hand, these programs are firmly set in the traditional classroom and would scarcely form the revolution we have been promised. Anderson[8] considers that

> Those developments which point the way forward are those which are in the business of providing learners with the *right* kinds of experience of computers. By the 'right' kind, I mean those which place the *learners* in control of learning, allowing them to make self-selecting decisions and to manipulate the informational substance of the discipline of knowledge being studied. Those developments to be discouraged are those in which the *teacher* uses the computer to constrain or to pace the learner or the learning, or to manipulate the knowledge base, denying the learner that experience of control.

A class–computer interaction forfeits the 'individualisation' which has always been claimed as one of the potential benefits of computer-assisted learning. It is not possible for these programs to perform actions designed to meet the educational needs of an individual student. With home computers becoming increasingly widespread I can see pupils become frustrated at the lack of 'hands-on' activity at school. I would worry too about the claims that using the computer as an aid 'demonstrates the capabilities of computers, improving understanding of them as well as of the subject taught'[9] and, soon after, that 'the computer may be used as another person', without qualification. Such glib anthropomorphisms will not help pupils (and teachers) over the widespread misconceptions that there already are about the capabilities of computers. Is it realistic to believe that really quite simple programs designed for another purpose could improve understanding of computers?

7. Giving Information

Having motivated, stimulated and activated the pupil, the computer must now give him some feedback about what he has done. In the case of drills, this could be by means of a response such as 'incorrect: the answer is X' (as with **Climate**). Or there could be no explicit answer—the feedback being implied by what happens on the screen (as with **Snooker** and **Janeplus**, which, in fact, never gives an 'answer'). In addition, there are programs which try to provide information appropriate to the perceived needs of the pupil. This is, in general, difficult to do satisfactorily but the evidence suggests that such feedback is more effective.

To take a specific example, consider multiplication. How should a program respond to this?

```
  64
× 9
----
 546
```

Some possibilities are:

1. 'Wrong.'
2. 'Wrong. The answer is 576.'
3. '4 times 9 is 36. So put down 6 and carry 3.
   6 times 9 is 54. 54 plus 3 is 57.
   So put down 7 and then put down 5.
   So the answer is 576.'
4. 'What is 4 times 9?'
5. 'You forgot to carry 3.'
6. 'What should you have carried?' (asked as soon as the pupil types the 4), and so on.

What evidence is there for preferring one form of feedback to another? Tait, Hartley and Anderson[1] showed many years ago that 'active' feedback (such as 6 above) is more effective than 'passive' feedback (such as 3 above). In addition, one would expect it to be better to provide feedback relevant to the pupil's particular difficulty (as in 5 and 6) than to plough through the same set of questions every time (as in 4). None the less, most existing multiplication drills give some variation on options 1–3 (because, of course, to do more requires a more detailed task analysis and greater programming skill). Would **Climate** be more effective if it first asked the pupil to classify a climate and, only in the event of a mistake, went through some of the preliminary questions? Maybe not, for there is no algorithm to classify climates as there is to do multiplication, and it is misleading to suggest that there is by presenting the topic as a drill.

Perhaps the basic ideas of climatology are better presented by a tutorial. In dialogues such as that shown in Figure 6.2 the computer's feedback is of statements entirely prespecified by the programmer. He must try to anticipate possible misconceptions by the pupil and to provide sensible 'remedial' messages. All too often, however, the pupil is bewildered by some supposedly helpful advice which is unrelated to his actual difficulties.

An alternative strategy is not to try to write programs which attempt to guess what the pupil needs but to write programs which enable the pupil to decide for himself what information he needs. In this case, the program designer must decide on ways of storing information in the computer's memory so that items can be retrieved sufficiently speedily, and on ways of enabling the user to specify items of information to be retrieved (and possibly to add new items). Such information retrieval systems are disinterested resources: they are not concerned with the 'worth' of any information stored or of any retrieval request. Information retrieval systems designed to be used by adults on large computers have existed for many years. Public information systems, such as *Prestel*, and micro-based systems designed to be used by children are more recent phenomena. Examples of the latter are **Factfile**,[2] **Leep**,[3] **Questd**[4] and **Sir**.[5]

To communicate with an information retrieval system the user must learn a 'query language', since it is not possible to write a program to understand free English. Designing a query language, like designing a programming language, requires considerable technical skill. The designers of **Factfile** attempt to circumvent the problem by using an entirely menu-driven interaction. Figure 7.1 gives part of a dialogue about a file of information on dinosaurs. For some reason, the designers believed that seven-year-olds would be happier with 'entry', 'item' and 'headings' instead of the usual jargon: 'record', 'key' and 'fields'. Is this laborious hand-holding more acceptable to children than using some conventional notation such as 'find (dinosaurs, diet=plant)', or even some pseudo-English such as 'Which dinosaurs had diet=plant?', which would not be too difficult to support? Designers continue to follow their own intuitions with little attempt to find evidence to support them.

Since a query language is only a special-purpose programming language, another solution might be to use an existing programming language as a query language. **Prolog** is a language which can be used to set up databases of information and to ask questions about a database. A more technical consideration of **Prolog** follows in Chapter 12; for the moment, I hope the rather baroque notation does not obscure the general point. In **Prolog**, the user can add facts and rules of inference to a database:

```
assert(mother(elizabeth,charles))
assert(parent(X,Y):-mother(X,Y))
```

i.e. X is a parent of Y if X is a mother of Y. The **Prolog** convention is to use capital letters for variables and small letters for constants, i.e. named things. The user can then ask questions:

```
parent(X,charles)
```

to receive the answer, if this were all the database contained,

```
X is elizabeth.
```

Ennals[6] describes how **Prolog** may be used to carry out 'historical simulations'. This involves establishing a database containing facts such as:

```
member(stalin,bolsheviks)
tactics(lenin,non-cooperation)
wants(X,revolution):-member(X,bolsheviks)
```

and then asking questions such as:

```
wants(stalin,Y)
```

```
Look at a file
You can

A   see all the DINOSAURS
B   see one DINOSAUR
C   ask something else
D   go back to the Choice Page

Press A B C or D
```
(Emma presses C and RETUR'

```
Look at a file

How many headings do you want
to look at?



Type it then press RETURN
```
(Emma types 2 and presses RETURN)

```
Look at a file

What is the 1st heading?



Type it then press RETURN
```
(Emma types DIET and presses RETURN)

```
Look at a file

What is the 1st entry?



Type it then press RETURN
```
(Emma types PLANT and presses RETURN)

```
Look at a file

You can see DINOSAURS with
DIET

A   the same as PLANT
B   not the same as PLANT

Press A or B
```
(Emma types A and presses RETURN)

Figure 7.1

to receive an answer:

```
Y is revolution.
```

To set facts in a historical context, they may be 'time-stamped' as in:

```
at(mobilises(russia,army),1914)
```

The purpose of the exercise is 'to facilitate judgement and decision on the part of the students [and] to extend their capacity to consider information.'

It is important for pupils to learn how to use computers to access information and to appreciate the value of the information so retrieved, for they will increasingly be required to do so in school and outside. Again, however, there are deep questions which educational software designers seem happy to ride roughshod over. Computers process representations of information—which is not the same thing as information, still less is it knowledge, and even less is it education. The sequence of symbols in 'Stalin died in 1953' is one representation of a piece of information. The same information could be represented in French or morse code and it would make no difference provided the decoding mechanism could interpret the sequence of symbols. Interpreting symbols involves more than transcribing them from one form to another, from morse '. . .' to the character 'S', say. It involved relating the symbols to previously 'understood' symbols—knowing who 'Stalin' refers to, that '1953' is a date, and so on. For humans, most of this is automatic: only when a representation is anomalous or ambiguous are we consciously aware of our attempts to interpret it. For computers (strangely?), it is not automatic. Sequences of symbols such as 'Stalin died in 1953' or 'died (stalin, 1953)' can be stored in a computer's memory and it can be arranged for the computer to answer 'when did Stalin die?' or 'died (stalin, X)' by matching the symbols in the latter, one by one, with those in 'died (stalin, 1953)' to respond 'X is 1953'.

But what has matching symbols to do with understanding who Stalin was, or what dying means? Are we to conclude that the computer's output is to be treated as an inherently meaningless sequence of symbols? Of course not, and the reason is that, in general, the computer's answers come from processing representations of any number of facts, using calculation, reasoning, analogy or other techniques the programmer has been able to provide. The computer's answer is meaningful to the extent that these representations and their interpreting mechanisms are meaningful. So, when the computer pronounces that 'Stalin wants revolution' we should appreciate that the computer 'knows' no more and no less about 'revolution' than is contained in its representations of relevant facts and rules of inference. If a pupil is involved in creating the contents of a database (and does not merely use one) then he is presumably more likely to understand this, but I doubt whether many children would be able to follow the complex reasoning involved in processing a worthwhile representation of the Russian Revolution.

This leads on to the question of just what facts can be represented in a computer's memory. Can *you* say precisely what a 'revolution' is? Of course, it is very difficult—an adequate answer requires some explanation of democracy, violence, justice, and so on. Any computer representation is bound to be a gross simplification. In addition, it is not just facts that need to be represented. We also need 'causation', a concept that has perplexed philosophers for centuries. 'Time', too, is difficult to handle satisfactorily by a computer program—the notation introduced above cannot be taken very far.

From these imperfect representations (and they become more imperfect as they become more interesting) pupils are expected to extract knowledge. As Hirst[7] remarks:

Knowledge must never be thought of merely as vast bodies of tested symbolic expressions . . . all knowledge involves the use of symbols and the making of judgements in ways that cannot be expressed in words and can only be learnt in a tradition. [In particular] the forming of a historical explanation and the assessment of its truth [is described as one of the] high arts that are not in themselves communicable simply in words. Acquiring knowledge of any form is therefore . . . something that cannot be done simply by solitary study of the symbolic expressions of knowledge.

'Information' can be given a precise mathematical definition, but of more use to us is Paisley's suggestion that information is 'any stimulus that alters the cognitive structure in the receiver . . . something that the receiver already knows is not information.'[8] Neither, we should add, is something that the receiver is unable to assimilate into his cognitive structure. 'Knowledge' is, in part, what results from the assimilation of information, or, as Bell[9] puts it, knowledge is 'an organised set of statements of facts or ideas, presenting a reasoned judgement or an experimental result.' Knowledge is more than information in two ways: some knowledge is information transformed in some manner, and some knowledge is not acquired from information (in the normal sense) at all: it may be acquired, for example, by 'experience'. And, of course, to be 'knowledgable' is not the same thing as to be 'educated'.

Computer technology is excellent for carrying out complex searches through vast bodies of (representations of) information. This awesome power can lend an unwarranted authority to its results. It is easy to overlook the fact that, educationally, the context in which an activity is carried out is much more important than the actual symbols displayed on the screen.

8. Encouraging Practice

Once a program has been written to perform some task it is a simple matter to modify it to get the task performed repeatedly. Consequently computer drills, in which a pupil is required to practise solving problems of the same type, are the most common form of educational software. They are also the most criticised.

Criticisms are of two sorts, pedagogical and technical. The number of computer drills is out of all proportion to the amount of worthwhile learning which can be achieved with them. Constant repetition of one activity rarely leads to the learning of concepts and principles, and the development of problem-solving strategies. Another meaning of 'to drill' is 'to bore' and this is also applicable. The prospect of generations of children being endlessly drilled by computers in tasks such as long division, fraction multiplication, climate identification, and so on, is so appalling that I assume no educationalist would countenance it for long.

None the less, there is a place for computer drills, but most are too badly designed to deserve it. Practice is necessary for learning verbal chains and associations, such as typing and spelling, and for consolidating understanding. *After* understanding has been achieved, practice may help build up confidence in using newly-learned skills. If, then, we accept that there are some situations in which computer drills may be useful, how should they be designed? Lesgold[1] gives three guidelines:

1. The environment should be motivating.
2. The tasks should be appropriate to the pupil's level of progress.
3. The tasks should provide understandable, productive and immediate feedback.

These guidelines seem so sensible, yet so imprecise, that they might almost be called platitudes. Let us look at some existing programs to try to pin down what is required.

Percents[2] (or '**120c**' as its publisher prefers to call it) is a program which carries out a drill on the conversion between fractions and percentages. It repeatedly asks questions either of the form:

```
P/Q expressed as a percentage =?
```

or of the form:

```
P percent converted into a fraction =?
```

where P and Q are integers. If the pupil answers either question incorrectly, he receives a hint of the form:

```
No, P/Q is (P/Q) X 100 percent,try again
```

or:

```
No, P percent is P/100. If top and bottom
of fraction are exactly divisible by the
same numbers then divide by these
numbers,try again
```

where P and Q are the letters themselves, not the integers that appear in the questions! If the pupil persists with a second wrong answer, he is told the correct one. After every fifth question the pupil gets a score (expressed as a percentage, naturally).

Considering Lesgold's three guidelines, first, you may judge for yourself whether this environment is likely to prove motivating. Secondly, is the task appropriate to the pupil's level of progress? The numbers that appear in the questions are generated at random—there is nothing built into the program which corresponds to the notion that 5/6 is harder to convert to a percentage than 1/4. Moreover, the numbers are not determined by how well or how badly a pupil is doing—the questions do not get any easier if the pupil is having difficulty. In short, **Percents** assumes (as most drills do) that a pupil comes to the program with just the right level of incompetence to benefit from practice and that this level will not change significantly while using the program.

Thirdly, the feedback that **Percents** provides is of two kinds: after the first mistake, a description of how to solve this kind of problem, and after the second mistake, the answer itself. As remarked in Chapter 7, passive feedback of this sort is not very effective. Determining an appropriate hint to offer a pupil is a subtle issue for it ought to depend on the particular problem presented and the pupil's particular difficulty.

For **Percents** to be able to give the answer and to recognise a pupil's input as right or wrong it would seem necessary for the program to be able to solve the problem it has generated. This is not the case for all drills for, as we saw with **Climate**, which selected problems rather than generated them, it is sometimes possible for the programmer to store all the answers to the questions. This was done for **Climate** because the programmer could not (or at least did not) write the algorithm to work out the answers. Sometimes, in fact, it is easy for a program to check whether or not a pupil's answer is correct but very difficult to work out the answer, for example, to calculate the root of some algebraic equation. **Percents**, of course, works out its answers when it needs them since the program to do so is easy to write. As **Snooker** showed, it is not always necessary for a program explicitly to label a pupil's answer as right or wrong. Indeed, there is at least one program[3] which does not even require the pupil to type in an answer: the pupil simply thinks the answer and after due cerebration asks the program to say what the answer actually is.

Having said that it is easy to write a program to convert between fractions and percentages, I must say that the **Percents'** programmer has tried to demonstrate otherwise and the limitations unnecessarily imposed are typical of those which buyers of educational software are expected to tolerate. The first problem he had was to decide what to do with decimal parts: was 2/3 to be 66.6, 67 or what? The decision was to ask the pupil to omit the decimal part and not round, so that 2/3 was to be 66 per cent: programming convenience overriding sound educational practice, perhaps? It would appear not, for, in coping with this, the programmer contrives to accept 61 per cent for 3/5 and 74 per cent for 3/4. Even though the pupil is not required to type in the decimal part, the program's version of the answer includes them. In addition, the text displayed on the screen is ungrammatical and so badly laid out that the pupil's answer of 3/50, say, is split over two lines. Such 'minor' inconveniences are all too common.

Computer drills can, of course, be enlivened by using some of the computer's other capabilities. **Trains**,[4] for example, is a straightforward drill on addition, subtraction and multiplication except that little pictures of trains accumulate in the corner of the screen as the pupil answers questions correctly (and some of them vanish if he makes a mistake). **Claws**[5] is a similar drill, but in this case a 'claw' moves threateningly across the screen to encourage the child to answer quickly. Failure to answer quickly enough leads to a graphical sequence more entertaining than that greeting success—as is often the case. **Bomber**,[6] winner of the 1982 Sinclair/MUSE Educational Award for Primary Maths, and described as 'definitely a cut above the vast majority',[7] is a multiplication drill in which the child is required to 'bomb' the correct answer out of a set of possible answers moving along the bottom of the screen. **Number Gulper**[8] is an arcade game that encourages children to practise arithmetic skills. The player has to steer a gulper to gulp numbers on the track in order to make a target number. These programs are, no doubt, fun to write and to play with, and only a spoilsport would point out that there is no evidence at all that the unadorned versions are not equally ineffective in promoting learning.

Let us now consider a much more substantial program, **Bertie**,[9] designed to help university students acquire the strategies and tactics needed to solve problems in natural deduction. A few preliminary words of explanation might be helpful. In a formal logical system there are rules of grammar which determine whether a particular sequence of symbols is a 'well-formed formula'. In **Bertie**'s case,

G=>[F=>(S&L)]

is well formed. There is also a set of 'rules of inference' for deducing a new formula from one or more other formulae. For example, for **Bertie** there is a rule, called *modus ponens*, which enables

F=>(S&L)

to be deduced from

G

and

G=>[F=>(S&L)]

The problem, generally, is to show that a particular formula can be deduced using the given rules of inference from a given set of formulae, the premises. Since there are a fair number of rules of inference and the number of formulae is liable to grow rapidly, it is usually not feasible to apply rules blindly in the hope that the theorem will be stumbled upon.

According to the designers of **Bertie**, 'the only way to develop a skill at constructing deductions is through practice at using the various rules.' So, in one mode of use, **Bertie** presents a formula to be deduced and the pupil has to type in each step of a proof (both the new formula deduced and the rule of inference and old formulae used to derive it). As each line is typed in, **Bertie** checks that the formula is well formed and that it actually follows from the rule and formulae cited. A set of fifty problems is provided, designed to give practice in all the rules and arranged in order of increasing difficulty. It is also possible for a pupil to enter his own problem.

Apart from the immediate notification of errors in typing formulae or in applying rules, **Bertie** provides help in three ways. First, a pupil unsure about a particular rule may ask for it to be applied to specified formulae. Secondly, if the pupil becomes stuck while trying to complete one of the fifty problems, he may ask for a hint or for the next few lines of a proof to be given. Thirdly, he may ask to be shown a complete 'canned' solution.

What more could one ask of such a drill? Well, **Bertie**, like **Climate**, cannot itself solve the problems which it expects its users to solve. **Bertie** can, therefore, only give pre-stored hints associated with the fifty problems (although, at least, they are different for different problems, unlike **Climate**'s hints). This confuses students, who do not realise that the hints are not related to what they have just done. **Bertie** can give no hints or help with problems typed in by the pupil. **Bertie** can only check proofs, it cannot generate them. As a result, **Bertie** cannot comment, except in an entirely predetermined way, upon the strategies and tactics which the pupil is using and which the program is intended to develop in the pupil. Should it, even if it could? Or would it be better to let a pupil discover for himself how to carry out proofs? It seems to me that the computer's infinite patience, often quoted as a virtue, may be harmful if it allows pupils to consolidate misunderstandings.

On the other hand, to insist that a computer drill should itself be able to do whatever it asks pupils to do will severely limit the number of drills which can be written. For example, it is a formidable task to write a program able to prove theorems. If drills are restricted to those tasks for which programs may easily be written, it is reasonable to wonder whether pupils need to learn how to do those tasks anyway. Even if we had a program able to prove theorems, we might still be far from providing the kind of understanding necessary to be able to comment upon strategies and tactics. There are many acceptable ways of carrying out a proof: the program's and the pupil's ways may differ, so how are they to be related? If the program's way is deemed to be the only acceptable way, how is this to be explained to the pupil? Programs able to explain themselves are not easy to write!

9. Sequencing Learning

All the programs discussed up to now could be described as 'closed' programs in that they are all designed to perform only one task and do not refer to any other program within a longer-term learning sequence. Present microcomputers, for which most of the programs have been written, do not encourage designers to be more ambitious than the small, self-contained 'package', for which there are problems enough.

However, some of the programs are designed to be adaptable for a range of pupil ability. Often this is achieved by allowing the teacher, or the pupil, to set the 'difficulty level' before the program proper is run. For example, **Trains** begins by asking the user to select the number of digits to appear in the problems presented. Many computer games, too, are designed to be played at various levels, the player selecting an appropriate one before starting.

It is natural next to wonder whether this could be automatic: that is, whether the program could itself determine a difficulty level appropriate to the particular user, and to adjust this level as the user's competence changes. Two programs on a tape distributed by Houghton County Primary School illustrate this idea. **Autoadd** is designed to reinforce the process of addition. It has eight levels, and the program automatically moves up a level if six examples are completed without error. The other, **Placevalue**, is a game designed to reinforce placevalue concepts. The player uses a defence ship to catch bombs (again) dropped by a flying saucer. As the number of bombs caught increases, the game speeds up.

Once the idea of a self-adjusting drill is accepted there is no limit (in principle) to the number of levels included and to the subtlety of the decisions for changing levels. This idea, however, is not a new one. The Stanford drills have been used since 1965 to teach hundreds of thousands of American children the basics of mathematics.[1] These drills are organised as strands, each of which includes problem types of a given concept (e.g. fractions, horizontal addition) and within each strand problems are grouped into classes. The particular problems presented depend on pupil performance, and greater emphasis is given to those strands on which he has a lower level of performance. His rate of progress through the classes of a strand depends on his ability to solve the problems set. Thus, unlike traditional classroom exercises, the Stanford drills enable each pupil to tackle a different set of problems, ideally ones appropriate to his level of ability.

This attention to the needs of an individual learner, rather than to those of an assumed homogeneous set of learners, was also one of the motivations for designing the branching programs discussed in Chapter 6. Some designers believe that 'tutorial programs which can be made really responsive to the individual student's needs are still the basis for the best in CAL.'[2] The difficulty, of course, is making them 'really responsive'.

The strategy of the **World War One** program (Figure 6.2), which is to present multiple-choice questions leading to the next frame or back to a previous frame, is one of the simplest possible. Another possibility is to have a main branch, with 'remedial branches' to deal with wrong answers. Any branching program requires the designer to anticipate the misconceptions that each response entails. If the question were one requiring the pupil to type in, rather than select, an answer (e.g. 'Which countries were members of the Triple Entente?'), then the designer's problems are increased for he has to anticipate reasonable, but wrong, answers and to think of a sensible response to each. To do the job properly, the question should be considered within the context of a tutorial discussion, not as an isolated question. So, if there are 100 frames to present and each frame branches to six other frames, then there are more than 10^{77} paths for the designer to ensure are sensible (assuming each frame is presented only once). Obviously, designers settle for less. In fact, the branching decisions are usually made on the basis of the pupil's last response only.

How is the branching decision made? When the pupil types in an answer then clearly this answer must be analysed. Often this analysis is shallow: the designer might write a piece of program which says, in effect, 'if the pupil types something which contains an approximation to the word "Tannenberg" then he has probably confused a battle site with the German general in charge.' This decision can be as intricate as the designer cares to make it, but, in practice, the rules are simple. Any mistake by the designer destroys the elaborate façade of comprehension. It is because the programs lack any significant understanding of the topics under 'discussion' that they have to be carefully designed to prevent pupils asking awkward questions, or, indeed, any questions at all. Moreover, the questions put to pupils have to be such as to have easily analysable answers, and consequently, tend to be superficial.

There is no hard-and-fast boundary between the stand-alone program, such as **Bomber**, for example, and the program, such as any in the Stanford series, designed to form part of an integrated, longer course. A teacher could, if he wished, build up a course around programs originally designed to be used separately. But if programs are intended to relate to one another, to some extent automatically, then a substantial exercise in educational design has to be faced. Some of the problems are illustrated by a computer-based statistics course designed at the University of Leeds.

It was found that the first versions of the programs were liked neither by students (who were required to spend an hour or more working at a terminal) nor by staff (who found that the extensive programs included topics, examples and contexts which they left out or taught differently). The programs were then rewritten as small, independent modules which could be collated by a lecturer into any desired sequence. In addition, the student was allowed to stop any session when he wished and the system would automatically resume from this point when the student returned. After two or three years, however, it was felt that the annual task of putting together specific courses was too time-consuming for the lecturers. Consequently, a higher-level language was developed to enable sequences to be defined more easily and for these sequences to be automatically converted into teaching programs.

It thus took several years to develop the 200 or more modules to a form in which they could be conveniently used. The programs eventually came into regular use with about 1000 students a year at the Universities of Leeds and Bradford and at Leeds Polytechnic. The computer-based materials were fully integrated in the various departments' statistics teaching, the programs serving as a statistical laboratory, giving illustrations of statistical concepts, and providing individualised teaching and guidance in problem-solving and experimental design. Alas, the programs, which were written in the days before visual display units, now look old-fashioned and have fallen into disuse.

While experience at designing such large-scale, integrated courses is accumulating, the high development costs ensure that they will be more attractive to commercial computer-based training developers with well-endowed clients. For example, WICAT Systems[3] describe training systems developed for American Express, British Telecom and the British Navy and Army. The teaching programs are developed using 'authoring systems' (described in Chapter 13).

These kinds of teaching system begin to merge with those generally described as 'computer-managed learning' systems. Here, the computer is not used directly to aid learning but is used to make administrative decisions about which modules or units (not necessarily computer-based ones) an individual pupil should be directed to. As far as the decision-making aspect is concerned, the distinction is simply one of scope. In computer-managed learning, decisions are what Maddison[4] calls 'strategic' ones (i.e. concerned with directing the larger operations of a campaign); in computer-assisted learning, they are 'tactical' (i.e. concerned with manoeuvring in the presence of the pupil).

To what extent is it reasonable to talk of the computer making decisions which sequence learning? Isn't the computer merely following a path prescribed by the program designer, just as a television presents material in the order prescribed by the programme producer? Clearly, when **Autoadd** 'decides' that a pupil should move up a level it is only following a criterion ('six correct in a row') prespecified by the designer. One obvious difference from the television programme, however, is that the decision is made while, not before, the learning activity is carried out. But there is a more fundamental difference. The 'six correct in a row' criterion is an easily tested behavioural measure standing in for the real criterion, which is a cognitive one, that, for example, 'the pupil has now understood how to do vertical addition of two-digit sums without carry.' While the decision has to be expressed in behavioural terms, that is, in terms of what the pupil actually does, the decision only makes sense in terms of what the pupil knows or understands. The program's test of understanding can be as complex as we wish. For determining whether the pupil understands something at all significant the test should be complex, weighing up all the relevant evidence that the program has accumulated. In fact, it may be so complex that the program designer may be unable to follow all of its ramifications. So, as with many complex programs, nobody will be able to predict exactly what decisions the program will make. In such a case, it seems reasonable to describe the computer as making autonomous decisions: certainly, pupils behave as though they believe the computer to be doing so.

10. Providing a Resource

Many educationalists will begin to rebel (if they have not done so already) at the suggestion that computers should be considered responsible for making decisions about teaching strategies. Using computers to reinforce the prevalent teacher-centred culture is bad enough: creating a computer-centred culture is going too far, they will say. If the aim of education is to aid the 'self-realisation of the individual' then education must be a learner-centred activity, and from this it will be argued that overtly didactic teaching and receptive learning is not to be encouraged. Instead, learners should be responsible for their own decisions about educational goals and should learn 'by discovery'. Now, arguments of this sort go to the heart of educational philosophy and it is not my purpose to pursue them to any depth. But if the computer can be considered as a third partner in the teacher – learner relationship, then clearly these arguments will become more complicated. So we must consider the extent to which a learner may use a computer as a resource to serve his own ends, independently of a teacher, and the extent to which this is likely to be beneficial.

Let us begin by looking at a program which, in a sense, must be used as a resource since it is delivered with absolutely no suggestions as to how it is to be used. According to its publishers, **Translate**[1] 'allows the pupil to create a shape and explore the effects of reflection, rotation or translation', but there are no accompanying notes explaining what the pupil or teacher should do with the program. On running the program, the pupil is confronted with a grid on the screen and he is then required to specify the coordinates of the end-points of lines of a shape to be transformed (Figure 10.1). He may then have the shape replicated to form a circular pattern (Figure 10.2), in which the number of replications is selected from a set of options (6, 10, 12, . . . 36). Alternatively, he may specify a shape to be reflected (Figure 10.3),

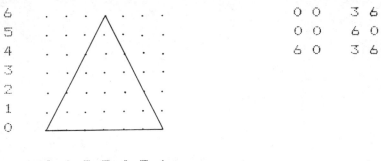

```
6    . . .  /\  . . .          0 0    3 6
5    . . ./ . \. . .          0 0    6 0
4    . . / .  . \. .          6 0    3 6
3    . / . . . . \ .
2    . / . . . . \ .
1    ./ . . . . . \.
0    /_____\
```

```
     0 1 2 3 4 5 6
```

Where would you like line 4 ?
Type in coordinates of first end
(or press 'ESC' if finished)

Figure 10.1

rotated (Figure 10.4) or translated (Figure 10.5). The pupil is then expected to look at the pattern until he has 'seen enough'.

What can a pupil do with this program? What kind of self-imposed project of educational value can he carry out? Imagine that the pupil is unhappy with the untidy appearance of the circular pattern (Figure 10.2) and prefers that shown in Figure 10.6. Can he create the latter using **Translate**? His first problem is

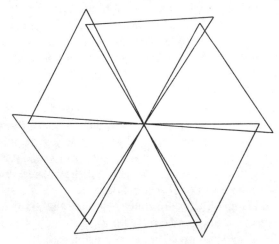

Figure 10.2

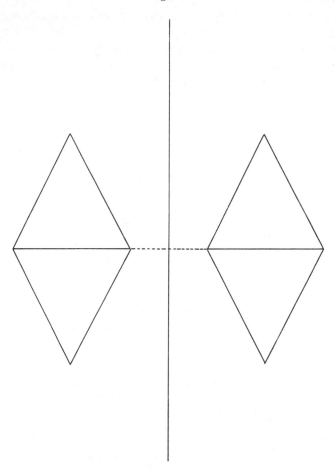

Figure 10.3

that having specified the basic shape (Figure 10.1) there is no way
to change it except by redefining the whole thing. This, of course,
is very tiresome but, however persistent the pupil is, he will never
create Figure 10.6 using **Translate** because it is not possible
to specify an equilateral triangle using the coordinate system
provided. Imagine, now, that our pupil decides to investigate what
rotation, reflection and translation mean. Again, he will not get
very far because to **Translate** they mean only one thing and there
is nothing the pupil can do about it. A 'rotation', for example,

means one through 90 degrees about the origin, and this cannot be changed.

Translate is only a small program, but it does serve to illustrate two points which apply equally well to more ambitious programs of the 'open-ended' type. First, designing such a program involves

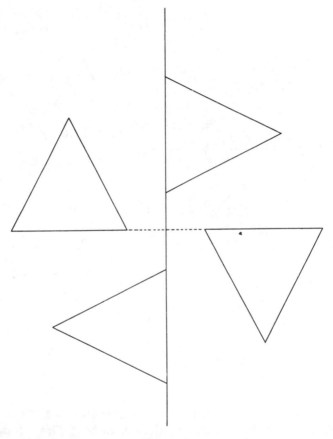

Figure 10.4

decisions about what to include and what not to include. This is particularly crucial for programs intended to aid discovery: how far should the designer go in aiding the learner towards discovery? Indeed, how does the designer avoid including features which obstruct discovery? In **Translate**'s case, are coordinates the best way to specify shapes? All educational programs are laden with value judgements, often made without due thought.

Secondly, designing a successful environment for discovery-learning involves considerable technical skill, more so even than the overtly didactic or teacher-controlled software looked at earlier. This is because the whole point of the exercise is to encourage free exploration. As a result, it is difficult to anticipate just what a pupil will decide to try to do, and consequently it is difficult to ensure that the pupil is not frustrated or obstructed by

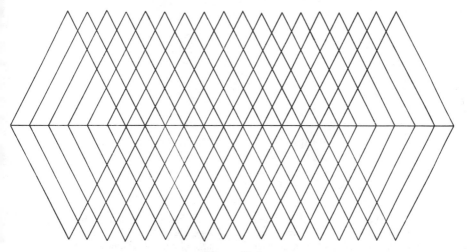

Figure 10.5

limitations of the program. With **Translate** no pupil will embark on a lengthy investigation because it is not possible to edit shapes quickly. Designing an editor which young children can easily use is a harder task than implementing the rest of **Translate**.

Logo is a programming language designed, among other things, to aid the drawing of patterns. In **Logo**, the pattern shown in Figure 10.6 may be created by first defining a procedure to draw a triangle:

```
To Triangle
    Repeat 3 [Forward 50 Right 120]
```
and then defining a procedure which uses the triangle procedure:
```
To Wheel
    Repeat 6 [Triangle Right 60]
```

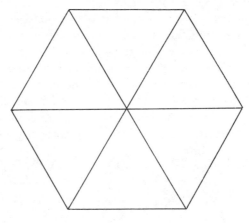

Figure 10.6

A call of the procedure 'Wheel' will result in the pattern being drawn. Let us assume (until Chapter 12) that **Logo** is technically a well-designed language which pupils are able to use without too much frustration, what then?

According to Lawler,[2]

> because **Logo** is a vehicle for free exploration, knowledge built from **Logo** is syntonic, appropriate to the person, and experienced as an authentic, intimate part of the self. Such is the power of an approach to learning that frees the individual to create within a social context that makes our culture's most powerful ideas accessible.

Logo, then, is also a vehicle for a philosophy of education and not a mere programming language. Some of the basic tenets of **Logo**-ology are:

1. Computer programming can be an arena for learning to learn.
2. Computers are general-purpose machines able to appeal to many different tastes.
3. Computer-based activities can support Piagetian, 'natural' modes of learning.
4. Computer power will soon be widely available in schools and homes.
5. The child should program the computer, not vice versa.

In short, the philosophy is opposed to the idea that the computer should be used to transmit suitably packaged knowledge to the learner.

It is a mistake to believe that **Logo**, or any more sophisticated derivative, provides a value-free environment for exploration. **Logo**, just like **Translate**, is not a natural object, but an artificial one created to serve some purpose. What has been included in **Logo** is a designer's decision based on educational and other objectives. One of the original objectives was that **Logo** should provide a 'conceptual framework for teaching mathematics'.[3] Of course, **Logo** would not be considered well designed if the objective were to provide a conceptual framework for teaching history, say. Even if we restrict ourselves to mathematics, then does **Logo**'s view of what mathematics is agree with that of most mathematicians? Obviously, **Logo** is not concerned with providing an even coverage of conventional mathematics curricula, for there are some parts of mathematics, such as matrix algebra, for which **Logo** would not be perspicacious. **Logo** is more concerned with fostering a style of learning mathematics.

It is idealistic, then, to say that with **Logo** children can freely explore mathematical ideas. Control of the real objectives remains with the designers of **Logo**. The child who decides to draw a wheel sets his own goal, but the **Logo** designer's objectives are set at a higher level. Lawler concedes as much by claiming that teachers/designers will 'achieve a kind of professional status long denied them' by using computer technology to create 'tools that will enrich our minds'. The question of who is really in control during **Logo** activities is complicated further by the fact that in many school projects using **Logo** it has been found necessary to develop rather conventional worksheets to guide the activities.[4]

The 'children programming computers, not computers programming children' slogan associated with **Logo**-ology is using the word 'programming' in two different senses, both unfairly. In the second phrase, 'programming' is used pejoratively to mean something akin to indoctrination: 'computers have conventionally been used in education to program the kids—in effect, to control their behaviour.'[5] I find it hard to see how most of the programs described earlier in this book could sensibly be described as programming children in the way suggested. In the first phrase, 'programming' is taken to refer to what many would regard as an advanced technical skill. The implication is that children are capable of acquiring 'a sense of mastery over a piece of the most modern and powerful technology'.

It seems to me that the ability of children to write computer programs has been exaggerated. Let us compare programming with the skill of composing music. All children can 'play the piano' in the sense that they can press the keys to obtain what is to them, at least, a pleasing noise. Most children of, say, seven can discover the sequence of keys necessary to play a familiar tune, such as 'Twinkle, Twinkle'. However, few children of any age can create lengthy musical compositions with a coherent structure and with an acceptable balance of melody, harmony and dynamics. Similarly, all children can press buttons to obtain pleasing drawings: many **Logo** systems for young children are provided with button boxes for just this purpose. Most children of, say, ten will with patience discover how to draw a wheel like that shown in Figure 10.6. But few children will be able to create lengthy programs making appropriate use of the full range of programming techniques. Unfortunately, all these activities are lumped together as 'programming'.

There is, in addition, a significant difference between composing music and writing computer programs. With the former, it is reasonably clear where you start: with a standard set of instruments and established conventions for specifying musical compositions. With the latter, writing a program to draw a wheel could range from specifying a very lengthy and detailed sequence of instructions in the 'machine language' which the computer is built to be able to execute directly, through to writing a single instruction, 'Wheel', for, if a designer thought it appropriate he could include an instruction to 'Wheel' in his language just as the **Logo** designers decided to include 'Forward' in **Logo**. Clearly, there is a considerable difference in the difficulty in writing these two programs, and children would learn quite different things from doing so. For **Logo** to be successful, it must include enough—but not too much—for pupils to achieve worthwhile objectives. If **Logo** as it stands does not give a pupil sufficient help then the language can be extended by providing a library of useful procedures. Alternatively, of course, a more appropriate language could be used, if one could be found. It is no solution, however, to use the most advanced programming language possible as this might reduce the need for the pupil to think sufficiently about the problem to be solved.

Documented evidence concerning children's ability to program is remarkably scarce. The most substantial body of data was accumulated by the MIT **Logo** project and published in 1978–9.[6] The project aimed to teach programming to sixteen 11-year-old pupils at Brookline School during 20–40 hours of hands-on experience. It was concluded that fourteen of the children could be said to have learned to program in that they had mastered a minimum core of four concepts (briefly: command, sequence, procedure and debugging). However, half the pupils mastered none of four more advanced concepts (loop, variable, conditional and interaction). These are simplistic summaries of a complex experiment but then so is the claim to have 'led hundreds of children to becoming quite sophisticated programmers'.[7] Solomon[8] considered that 6–7-year-olds could use the following skills in **Logo** programming (planning, using procedures, using parameters, debugging, defining procedures without parameters) but gave few details.

Should these children's achievements count as 'programming'? I would hesitate to apply the term to the activity of specifying a sequence of steps (no matter how lengthy or how well broken down into logical units) which, when executed, always produce the same result (i.e. the program is just a notation for a sequence of button-pushes). 'Programming', to me, implies (at the least) anticipating a variety of conditions which might arise while a program is being executed, and specifying an appropriate reaction to them. It implies, then, understanding how to use a 'conditional' instruction (often of the form 'if . . . then . . . else . . .'), which in turn implies understanding the concept of a 'variable', i.e. the idea that a symbol stands for a value which is unknown at the time when the program is being created. In short, 'programming' involves a form of abstract reasoning, which Piaget considered is generally not available to a child until he reaches the age of eleven or so. As we might have expected, the Brookline 11-year-olds were just on the verge of mastering the concept of a conditional instruction. Those who claim, for example, that 'a five-year-old can program with **Logo** in his or her first few minutes at a keyboard'[9] must explain clearly what this means.

Let us now consider how programming, whatever form it takes, could help learning. Programming aids the development of problem-solving skills, especially if, as with **Logo**, the language encourages good techniques, such as dividing a large problem into smaller pieces, and provides an environment in which experimental solutions can be easily tested. This is so almost irrespective of the particular problem provided, of course, that it is one which the pupil actually wants to solve.

Sometimes, however, the learning objectives centre on the actual problem itself. For example, a child may embark on an animation of a dancing man partly, at least, to clarify his own understanding of dance routines. Does writing a program to do X aid understanding of X? Lord Kelvin, the engineer, claimed that he could not understand anything until he had built a mechanical model of it. Is it possible today to say we have not really understood something until we can build a computational model of it? Even if we restrict ourselves to the purely algorithmic, there are processes which are fairly easy to carry out but quite difficult to program, such as long division as carried out with pencil and paper. In this case, the programming difficulties arise mainly in screen layout rather than the algorithm itself. So trying to write a program to do long division would probably obscure understanding.

There are also processes which correspond to tacit knowledge, that is, processes which we carry out subconsciously and the performance of which would deteriorate if rules were consciously applied—remember the poor centipede who fell in a ditch trying to work out how he walked. It seems unlikely to me that all worthwhile knowledge is, even in principle, expressible in an explicit form, such as statements in a computer program. This point, of course, has been argued in depth by philosophers.[10] If we encourage pupils to make their knowledge explicit as computer programs they might conclude that knowledge which they cannot make explicit in this way is not worth having.

Are there any other unfortunate side-effects from this emphasis on the programmable? **Logo**-ologists emphasise the role of 'debugging': 'teaching and learning are not a matter of being wrong or right, but rather a process of debugging.'[11]

> The road to wisdom?
> Well, it's plain and simple to express:
> Err and err and err again
> But less and less and less.[12]

The contrast with much schoolwork, which is festooned with ticks and crosses, and with most computer drills is a valuable one, but the suggestion that programming should proceed by the progressive elimination of bugs is not one with which most programming theorists would agree. The problem with this style of programming is that you can rarely be sure that you have found the last bug. For serious programming, a style which tried to ensure that there are no bugs in the first place is recommended, and various advanced and necessarily mathematical techniques have been developed to enable programmers to prove that their programs are correct. Of course, children are not doing 'serious programming', but if they should move on to do so they will surely bring with them the style they have already learned.

Programming, if it is to mean anything at all, is a time-consuming activity. At some stage, a judgement will have to be made as to whether this time is productively spent. Meanwhile, the 'whizz-kid' compulsive programmer is becoming increasingly familiar. Some adolescents are entranced by their own ability to create artificial, yet totally controllable, worlds. They will work late into the night, forsaking all 'normal' activities, programming yet another imaginative computer game.

Of course, **Logo**-like activities do not necessarily lead to such unhealthy escapism, and yet one must wonder just how many hours a day **Logo** enthusiasts envisage children of the future will spend communicating with computers. We must accept that we are entering a 'computer culture'. Children will grow up in a society in which computers will be widely used. Naturally, children must learn something about how computers work and what can be done with them, but if children are to learn mathematics 'naturally' by communicating with 'mathematics-speaking beings'[13] (i.e. computers) as French children learn French by living in France, must they spend as much of their time in

Computerland as French children do in France? Presumably, we shall eventually have 'physics-speaking beings', 'ethics-speaking beings', and so on, all demanding their share of a child's time. No matter how technology transforms computer hardware, this scenario seems utterly alienating.

PART 3

Designing Educational Software

In Chapters 11–16 I shall discuss the various stages involved in the production of educational software. For reasons which will be discussed in Part 4, the present poor quality of educational software is usually blamed on the programmer and there is today, quite rightly, more concern for educational issues rather than technical ones. Educational computing is about education, not computing. While it must be conceded that educational questions are the most important ones, there are, alas, few answers to those questions—or rather, each teacher and each pupil seems to have his own answer. It is this need to cater for a wide range of attitudes to education which makes the design of educational software particularly difficult. Consequently, educational software designers should be making much greater use of programming skill, not less.

11. Designing Software

Before considering what is special about educational software, let's look at how any piece of software is produced. The following seven major stages can be identified:

1. analysis of requirements;
2. writing a specification;
3. designing the program;
4. implementing the program;
5. testing the program;
6. debugging the program;
7. publishing the program.

These stages tend to overlap, of course, and few products will pass smoothly through all stages—testing, for example, may reveal ambiguities in the specification, parts of which may then have to be rewritten, and so on.

Now to elaborate on each of the seven stages. Analysing the requirements is always the most important stage for it is the one which justifies the other six. It is also the one most often skimped. For educational software, this stage involves trying to provide answers to questions such as: What would the user be expected to learn from the program? How would the program fit into existing curricula? What would be the teacher's role while the program is being used? What would the program add to what could be done by other means? Is the program likely to be technically feasible? As these questions suggest, there is an important stage preliminary to the actual design process, that is, in coming up with an idea or proposal for a program. Sometimes this idea will come directly from a perceived educational need, sometimes it will be inspired by another program, but often the source of the idea (as with any idea) will not be easily traceable. At all events, the analysis of requirements should convince designers that this idea can be turned into a program to solve a real problem.

On the basis of this analysis, a precise specification should be written. This is a statement of what the program should do (not how it should do it). For commercial software developers, the specification will be part of the contract between those who require the software and those who are to develop it. It will often be a technical document longer even than the eventual program itself. Educational software designers frequently dispense with the specification. This may be because the same people are involved throughout all stages and it seems unnecessary to produce a contract with oneself. However, the prime function of the specification is not a legal one: it is to clarify what the program is to do. Perhaps, in recognition of the fact that nobody really knows what educational programs should do, the specifications for educational software may be permitted to be a little less precise than usual, but certainly they should be written.

I shall say a little more about designing and implementing the program later but, briefly for now, 'design' involves deciding on the overall structure of the program and on the particular algorithms to be used, while 'implementation' involves converting this design into a working program, that is, by 'coding' the algorithms in an appropriate programming language. Incidentally, the term 'programmer' should not be equated with 'coder' (as it often is, disparagingly) but should be used in a broad sense to include anyone directly involved in the detailed specification, design and development of software.

A program is tested to ensure that it meets its specification. The program is run with carefully chosen test data for which the results are known, and the program's output compared with these results. Because it is possible to test the program with only a tiny fraction of its possible input data (unless it is a very simple program), the test data have to be chosen with skill. Techniques for doing this do exist but they are not well developed.[1] As a result, testing can be very time-consuming, contributing (with its corollary, debugging) as much as half of the total development time, according to some estimates.[2] This is an absurdly high proportion of the time spent on 'non-productive' work and indicates that there is something seriously amiss with the preceding stages of software development. To escape from the wasteful cycle of code–test–debug, a more formal approach has been advocated, and I shall say more about this shortly.

So testing is difficult, but unfortunately it is even more so with educational software and takes on a rather different character. This is because, as noted above, there is often no specification against which the program can be tested. Educational software may be developed in an 'experimental' fashion: instead of using a specification to prescribe what a program should do, a program is written to a looser specification, tried out with teachers and pupils, and then modified according to their reactions. 'Testing' then becomes a crucial, constructive stage of the design process. In the absence of generally accepted precise 'theories of education' to guide software design, this seems a sensible way to proceed, but it does, of course, further lengthen development time and calls for greater programming skill in writing code which can be easily modified in the light of user-reactions. In addition, techniques have to be developed for accumulating and assessing these reactions.

'Debugging' is the process of removing 'bugs' found by testing so that the program does meet its specification. Since a 'debugged' program also needs testing, and since one can rarely demonstrate by testing that there are no more bugs, debugging is a process that ends only when it is thought uneconomic to look for further bugs. So, unless a program has been proved correct, a 'finished' program may still, at a later date, reveal more bugs. Removing bugs discovered after some official finish to a program's development is euphemistically called 'maintenance'. A program is also 'maintained' if it is subsequently modified to cover situations not anticipated in the original specification—for example, if the program is changed to run on a different computer. Again, maintenance of educational software is liable to form a more significant part of the whole process than it does for other software because users are only just beginning to appreciate what it is reasonable to expect of educational software and so are increasingly asking for existing programs to be extended to meet further needs.

Unless a program is intended to be used by only one person (and there is a place for such programs, albeit an expensive one), a program must be published in some way, that is, made available for general use, possibly for profit. This usually means that documentation must be written to accompany the program. In Chapter 16, I shall consider the publication of educational software only in so far as it differs from the publication of other educational material.

In summary, then, software design is a complex process, and educational software is particularly complex. There is, moreover, a further complication. Not only may individual stages be carried out by more than one person (for example, if it is a large program, parts of it may be written by different programmers) but the different stages may well be carried out by people skilled in different areas. The analysis of requirements for educational software should naturally be carried out by educationalists, and so should the testing of programs in classrooms. Consequently, there is a communication problem, particularly acute for educational software because the personnel involved have non-overlapping areas of expertise.

Now, some producers of educational software will not recognise all this as a description of their own activities. If a teacher writes a small program entirely for his own use then, of course, some of these stages need not be carried out thoroughly. Bawtree[3] considers that 'Some of the best programs, from the point of view of teaching aids and general usefulness in the classroom, are the shortest', and defines 'short' as '20 lines or thereabouts' of **Basic**. (To put this in perspective, **Percents** is 51 lines long, **Newton** is about 700, and **Bertie** about 2000.) Bell[4] agrees: 'only if several alternative schemes are offered within a program, or too much text displayed, need a program be longer than about 40 lines.' Short programs are, naturally, cheaper to develop and easier to understand and adapt, but let us not pretend that 40-line **Basic** programs will yield the promised revolution in education. At least school micros are now large enough not to provide a cloak for those not able to write larger programs anyway, and if short programs really are to be preferred then it will be on pedagogical, not technical, grounds.

I am convinced that any significant educational software entails a substantial design effort. This effort is not proportional to the size of the program. If it takes one day to write a 20-line program, it will almost certainly take much longer than 100 days to write a

2000-line program. This is because the lines are not independent. As the program grows, so the complexity of the interdependencies between lines is liable to explode. The programmer's main skill is in controlling this complexity. Much as the typical educational software designer today may wish it were not so (for he is technically untrained and gets his programs to work, if at all, by tinkering with them until they appear to pass certain tests), this skill is based upon an extensive scientific and mathematical foundation.[5] Why this skill is not now brought to bear on educational software (or, indeed, much other software) is discussed in Part 4.

The general recognition that programming is a difficult task is often dated as occurring at a 1968 conference at which the term 'software engineering' was chosen to express 'the need for software manufacture to be based on the types of theoretical foundations and practical disciplines that are traditional in the established branches of engineering.'[6] Anyone familiar with present software, especially educational software, will smile at the suggestion that programming is an engineering discipline. But this is to react to the products of programmers most of whom would be considered underqualified in any other engineering discipline. Programming is certainly 'engineering' in that it is concerned with the economical design of a tangible product of practical value. Whether or not there are substantial theoretical foundations to programming is a subjective judgement. As I have said, my judgement is that there are.

Would-be programmers are peculiarly reluctant to accept that there is a body of relevant knowledge they should master, and it would be an interesting study to determine why. It is as if a maker of paper planes refused to accept that aeronautics might be useful if he wanted to build real planes! This is not a computer science text but, as a test, here are a few fundamental concepts which professional programmers find useful: BNF, coroutine, finite automaton, garbage collector, inverted file, lexical analysis, loop invariant, NP-completeness, pattern matching, recursive descent, semaphore, and stack. (You decide whether you pass!) There are, of course, many more concepts and more advanced ones, and in addition a programmer needs project planning skills much like those needed for other engineering tasks.

Present-day programming, especially on micros, is distracted by a necessary concern for temporary technical trivia, a knowledge of which is then taken to be of general applicability. Three-day courses on the arbitrary details of a particular computer or language reinforce the belief that this knowledge is important and sufficient. While the lack of programming competence is only one of many obstacles facing educational software design, it is one which will not be overcome by the brute-force approach of training large numbers of people in superficial skills.

I shall end this chapter by looking briefly at just one well-developed area of computer science which most educational software designers seem to feel able to ignore. This concerns 'data structures' which, according to Wirth,[7] are one of the two main components of programs (the other being algorithms). A data structure is constructed in a regular way from components which are data objects. For example, a 'string' is a data structure which is a sequence of characters, and an array is an ordered collection of objects all of the same type, such as integers. These two data structures are all that **Basic** provides, but most modern programming languages provide convenient ways of processing more powerful data structures such as trees, graphs, lists, records or any other structure that is thought useful for the problem at hand. Of course, any data structure can be created in **Basic**, but it is inconvenient and therefore avoided.

Two simple examples of the use of data structures are **Animal** and **Adventure**. The well-known **Animal** program began life as a demonstration of the concept of a binary tree search. In fact, if this concept is understood, the game can be played quite well without a computer. With **Animal**, pupils answer questions asked by the program to guide it down branches of the tree to a leaf (Figure 11.1). This program, according to Poulton,[8] exercises the following thinking skills: 'questioning techniques, attribute testing, classifying, logical reasoning, thinking of possibilities, fluency, flexibility, reinforcing originality, curiosity, evaluating, together with the skills of knowledge'.

Adventure, stripped of its romance, is merely a traversal of a labelled directed graph. This is all that remains when the specific scene descriptions are removed so that pupils and teachers can

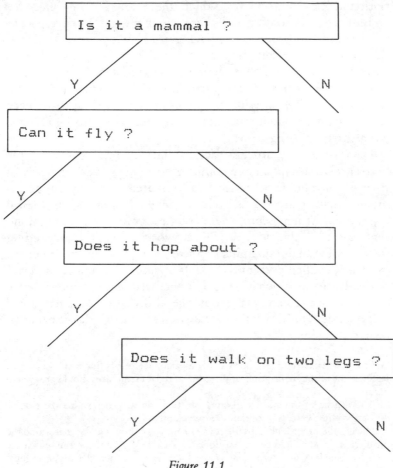

Figure 11.1

create their own environments to be explored, as has been proposed.[9]

In these two programs the need for data structures is obvious, however they are implemented. Sometimes programmers embark on programs without appreciating that their task would be much easier (and their products more useful) if appropriate data structures were used. A drill on symbolic differentiation (included with **Percents,** discussed in Chapter 8) illustrates the point. Without digressing to explain why it is worth doing, differentiation is an operation for which there are precise rules, for example, differentiating x^n (where n is an integer) with respect to x gives nx^{n-1}, differentiating $y \times z$ gives $z \times y' + y \times z'$ (where y' is the result of differentiating y; and similarly for z'), and so on. Symbolic differentiation is often one of the first examples given to illustrate the virtues of 'list-processing'.[10] This particular drill uses strings in **Basic**! As a result, the program can only deal with a very limited class of arithmetic expression, and cannot recognise two expressions as being equivalent.

Data structures are abstractions intended to emphasise the logical relationships among components of data, independently of their detailed implementation in a computer. Similarly, programming structures are abstractions intended to emphasise the logical relationships among components of a program. Wirth's opinion[11] that 'the adaptability of a program to changes in its objectives (often called maintainability) and to changes in its environment (nowadays called portability) can be measured primarily in terms of the degree to which it is neatly structured' is interesting in view of the above comments about the difficulties of educational software design. In fact, the conclusions of Wirth's classic paper all bear repeating:

1. Program construction consists of a sequence of refinement steps. . . . Refinement of the description of program and data structures should proceed in parallel.
2. The degree of modularity obtained in this way will determine the ease or difficulty with which a program can be adapted. . . .
3. During the process of stepwise refinement, a notation which is natural to the problem in hand should be used as long as possible. The direction in which the notation develops is determined by the language in which the program must ultimately be specified. . . . This language should therefore allow us to express as naturally and clearly as possible the structures of program and data which emerge during the design process. . . .
4. Each refinement implies a number of design decisions based upon a set of design criteria. Among these criteria are efficiency, storage economy, clarity, and regularity of structure. . . .
5. The detailed elaborations on the development of even a short program form a long story, indicating that careful programming is not a trivial subject.

12. Programming Languages

If the user of an educational software package is happy with the product then the programming language in which it is written is irrelevant to him. Unfortunately, users rarely are completely happy with educational software products: programs are thought too expensive; they are often delivered late; they contain bugs; they run too slowly; and they just do not do what the user would like them to do. Many of these failings can be traced back to limitations imposed by the programming language used. Also, as was emphasised in Chapters 7 and 10, all educational programs require pupils to communicate in a restricted language, which may in fact be a fully-fledged programming language such as **Prolog** or **Logo**. For these two reasons, it is necessary to look briefly at the design of programming languages for education.

Whereas the design of a particular program proceeds from the abstract to the details by a process of refinement, programming language design proceeds by abstraction, that is, by generalizing from particular programs those features that should be provided directly in a programming language. The aim is to ease the programmer's task by relieving him of the need to seek ways of expressing things that could be standard. This process of abstraction is not simply a pragmatic one. It is guided by the programming language designer's intuitions about what should be provided to increase the reliability and intelligibility of programs, and by various underlying models of computation. I shall illustrate this by looking at the origins of several programming languages.

Wirth's concerns, summarised in the previous chapter, leads to a style of programming involving the writing of small, independently understandable modules (or procedures), and to an emphasis on the correctness of programs. The language he designed, **Pascal**, is a 'block-structured' language, with the procedure the main conceptual unit. For each construction in the language, there is a proof rule expressed in a special logic. Each rule defines the meaning of a construction and enables the programmer (in principle, anyway) to prove that his program is correct, that is, its results accord with the specification. A formula in this logic is written in the form

{P}S{Q}

which means 'if P is true and S is executed, then if S terminates, Q is true'. Details of the proof rules and their use are given in Alagic and Arbib.[1] Other programming languages guided by the desire to provide usable proof rules are **Euclid**, **Modula** and **Ada** (the proposed standard for US defence programs).

The similarity in the role of programming structures and data structures, noted in Chapter 11, had been implicitly recognised many years before in the design of **Lisp**. This language has an abstract syntax defined as a data structure of the language. Just as one can write, in **Lisp** notation,

```
(Stalin Member Bolsheviks)
```

and write a piece of program to interpret this notation in a required manner, so one can write, in the same notation,

```
(Wants-revolution
    (Lambda (X)
        (Match '(X Member Bolsheviks))))
```

to represent a procedure to be interpreted by the **Lisp** interpreter. So a **Lisp** program can be processed like any other datum, and this demonstrates that the distinction between programs and data necessary with most other programming languages is an artificial one. The 'Lambda' occurring above is a reminder that **Lisp** is based upon the 'lambda calculus', a logical formalism developed in the 1930s to model the mathematical notion of substitution of values for variables. Any computable function may be written as an expression in the lambda calculus, which has thus served as a basis for theoretical work on computational semantics. More practically, **Lisp**, with its emphasis on the processing of lists as universal data structures, has inspired the design of other languages, such as **Pop2** and **Logo**.

A logical system of similar vintage, combinatory logic, is the theoretical foundation for 'functional programming', a style of programming which dispenses with variables, and expresses programs as compositions of functional operators. The first language of this class was **Apl**, defined in 1962 and still with its enthusiastic users. Recently, functional programming has been proposed to liberate us from the 'von Neumann style',[2] that is, from the style of programming imposed by conventional programming languages based on the von Neumann concept of a computer as a processor, store and connecting 'tube'. Researchers hope that functional programming languages will have more useful properties for reasoning about programs.

Functional programmers are closely related to the 'logic programmers', who write their programs in a notation based on predicate logic. In **Prolog**, for example, a procedure corresponds to a rule of inference expressed as a predicate logic formula. These rules are invoked by a process of unification (similar to pattern matching), and the whole program, which consists of a set of such rules, is executed by automatically backtracking to find those rules, if any, which provide an answer to a question posed as a predicate logic theorem to be proved.

Basing a programming language on an established formal theory helps to provide a unity or elegance which aids the comprehension of programs written in those languages. Some programming languages are based on quite different models from those derived from classical mathematics. For example, **Smalltalk** is derived from a 'message-passing' model of computation, which stresses the communication between independent computing agents (sometimes called 'actors').

Other programming languages are not based on any formal model but are designed to ease the problem of executing a program on particular computer hardware. For example, some of the apparent oddities in the design of **Fortran** can be traced back to features of the hardware of the IBM 704, for which it was designed in about 1956. **Basic** was designed in 1965 as a simplified, interactive version of **Fortran** to be used by college humanities students. The idea of an interactive language (i.e. one in which the programmer gets an immediate response to what he types at a terminal, rather than one in which he submits jobs to be processed by a computer later), was something of a novelty in 1965, but **Basic** was not the first such language (this honour being assignable to **Joss**). In fact, **Basic** is unique among widely-used languages in not contributing a single new concept to programming language design.

Let us now concentrate on languages of particular relevance to educational computing, beginning with **Basic**, the language in which most educational software is written. **Basic** has been criticised before, and it will be again, but it has made little difference: it is now entrenched as the standard language for educational software. Most designers of educational software are not very interested in arguments about the merits of various languages. They have a job to do, and **Basic** is the only way to get it done. Unfortunately, **Basic** is already proving to be a disaster for the future of educational software.

First, we must consider how **Basic** ever became the standard. If a program is to be widely distributed, as it must be to reduce its cost, then the program must be executable on as many computers as possible. Since **Basic** is a simple language it is easy to provide, for each different make of computer, a way of executing programs written in it. So, if a program is written in **Basic** for one computer, it should be straightforward to transfer this program to a second computer. This, for example, is how Lewis (then director of the Computers in the Curriculum project, which produced **Newton** and other programs) rationalised the choice of **Basic** in 1971: 'Many special simulation languages have been designed for particular machines, but . . . these may preclude the wide use of the packages.'[3] Then, when the first microcomputers appeared, **Basic**, being the simplest language, was the first to be implemented. Today, **Basic** is almost synonymous with programming on micros, and for many common micros no alternative is provided. This tendency for the first, but primitive, product to become established has been called the 'QWERTY phenomenon',[4] by analogy with the way the original keyboard arrangement on a typewriter, intended to minimise key jams, has become standard. (The lesson of the analogy still holds even though there is little evidence that this is why the keyboard was so arranged![5])

Short programs, of the kind discussed in Chapter 11, look much the same in most languages, and perhaps **Basic** can be tolerated for these. It is mainly with larger programs that the virtues of good language-design matter. None the less, a little **Basic** extract may demonstrate some of the problems:

```
3300 G1 = G1 + D * S
3310 H1 = H1 + W * D
3320 S2 = S
3325 W2 = W
3330 R = SQR (G1 * G1 + H1 * H1)
3335 L = Z * ( SGN (G1)) / 2
3340 IF H1 < > 0 THEN L = ATN(G1 / H1)
3350 GOSUB 3400: REM CHECK QUADRANT
3355 S = S + D * - 1 * K * G1 / R / R / R
3360 W = W + D * - 1 * K * H1 / R / R / R
3375 S4 = SQR ((S + S2) * (S + S2)
            + (W + W2) * (W + W2)) / 2
```

This is the part of **Newton** which corresponds to the program outline given in Chapter 5. Can you see how to carry out the modification suggested there (to change r^3 to r^2)? It is fairly easy, but the extract is not as readable as it could be. What, for example, is L? Now picture this extract 'buried' among several hundred other lines of **Basic**, from which it is not protected (i.e. these lines are free to change the values of variables such as G1 and D). Clearly, the limitations of **Basic** (such as meaningless variable names and 'open' procedures) make such programs unnecessarily difficult, and hence time-consuming and costly, to develop and to modify.

Some of these limitations are self-imposed. For example, the **Newton** programmer has restricted himself to a subset of **Basic**, so-called **Minimal Basic**, in the hope that this subset, at least, will be common to many computers. So more meaningful variable names, such as 'ANGLE' (which is what the 'L' above is), are avoided because not all **Basics** allow them to be used. Not only have we to use the simplest programming language but a subset of that! Worse still, the strategy did not work, for the Computers in the Curriculum project had to abandon the attempt to rewrite some of their programs for new micros as it proved too difficult.[6]

The problems with non-standard **Basics** have been recognised for some time. The patent inadequacies of **Basic** tempt all implementers to add their own improvements, and it is in the manufacturers' interests to claim better 'extended' **Basics**. The result is an endless proliferation of incompatible **Basics** making transferability elusive. The American National Standards Institute (ANSI) began in 1974 an attempt to define a standard for **Basic**. At the time of writing (February 1984), it has yet to report. If the present proposal[7] is accepted and generally followed, it will immediately make a large proportion of existing programs non-standard. For example, spaces will be required around key-words—this is a consequence of allowing multi-character variable names—so that FORN=1TOM, now ingrained in the programming habits of a generation, must be written as FOR N = 1 TO M. However, there is little chance that a **Basic** standard will be generally followed, which is a pity, for if it were **Basic** would more quickly become the fossil it should be.

There may be one or two readers, unfamiliar with **Basic** lore, who are wondering why programmers should render their programs unreadable by not using spaces. The answer is simply that **Basic** programs often have to be shoe-horned into the memory of present micros and, because of the way **Basic** is usually implemented, each space 'wastes' one byte of memory. Wells[8] gives (with an appropriate warning that some of them are very undesirable in terms of program structure and readability) a list of 38 hints for decreasing the memory occupied by and increasing the running speed of **Basic** programs. Just three of these seem generalisable to other languages. None the less, such nuggets are regarded as quintessential programming wisdom by many **Basic** programmers.

Why do **Basic** programmers put up with the slow running-speed of **Basic** programs caused by their being interpreted, not compiled? (i.e. they are executed by repeatedly scanning and 'interpreting' each character of the program text, rather than by being converted once into machine instructions which are carried out much faster.) Interpreters have advantages for incomplete, undebugged programs; compilers are better for complete, de-bugged programs. In which of these two categories are educational software products supposed to lie?

Basic was not intended for writing even modest-sized programs for practical use—it was designed for beginners to write small programs. Is there any evidence that it does at least fulfil this role? Yes, of course: millions of beginners have written small programs in **Basic**. This, however, is no evidence that **Basic** is better suited for this, or any other role, than other programming languages.

Recently, **Basic**'s claim to be the beginner's language has been challenged by **Logo**, which is not a new language (in fact, it is almost as old as **Basic**) but has only just become available on micros. In 1980, Jones[9] considered that **Basic** was 'ideal for primary school use and is excellent for beginners': two years later, we find '**Logo** is the ideal thing for primary schools.'[10] No programming language is 'ideal', for all compromise a whole set of conflicting requirements. An uncritical devotion to any language has no place in educational computing. **Logo**, as we shall see, is an improvement on **Basic**, but it too has its limitations.

Let us look first at Harvey's[11] statement that **Logo** is a 'language for learning'. He identifies three ways in which this is so:

1. **Logo** is 'tuned' for interesting applications. This refers mainly to turtle graphics, the idea most associated with the **Logo** language. The turtle is a mechanical device which can be made to move across the floor, or a conceptual device which can be driven around a screen. The turtle is moved by issuing commands such as 'Forward 50' (as indicated in Chapter 10). Using this approach, rather than one based on coordinates, it is easier for beginners to create drawings.

2. **Logo** is user-friendly—it gives more polite and helpful error messages than most other languages, and supports a display editor for the interactive development of procedures. (It would be an interesting piece of research to determine the extent to which beginners can cope with present editors.) These, however, are features of the **Logo** operating system rather than the language itself. More relevant is the belief that **Logo** commands, such as 'Make "X :X + 1', are more intelligible than those of other languages, such as 'X = X + 1'. 'User-friendly' is not a precisely defined, technical term which can be applied categorically (or not) to a language. It will be considered further in Chapter 14.

3. **Logo** has no threshold and no ceiling. This is taken to mean that '**Logo** is easy enough for anyone to use, but powerful enough for any project.' Regarding the first part, this depends on what is meant by 'to use', as discussed in Chapter 10. The second part is actually vacuous, since all programming languages are equivalent, in that any program which can be written in one language can be rewritten in another, in principle. What is really meant is that it is easier in **Logo** for pupils to move on to more advanced projects because **Logo** is not a 'toy' language.

Is it sensible to design a programming language to be used by pupils of any age, from 4-year-olds to adults, as **Logo** has been? I hope it is not suggested that 4-year-olds will grow up with **Logo**, and so use it into the next century! Pupils should surely use languages suited to their age and ability. Few primary school-children will use list-processing commands, so why include them in versions of **Logo** intended for young children? Since full **Logo** implementations do not allow users to prune features they do not want, we have a flock of mock turtles, that is, subsets of the full **Logo** with only the turtle graphics commands. Provided these subsets are soundly implemented they seem to me to be entirely welcome for, apart from making pedagogical sense, they are cheaper, faster and smaller than full **Logo**s. Of course, serious **Logo**-ologists regard them with disdain.

Logo proper can be described as an interactive, procedural, list-processing, untyped, extensible programming language. Let's take each adjective in turn.

Interactive: **Logo**, like **Basic**, is interactive and so usually interpreted, not compiled. This is acceptable, for **Logo** is intended to be suited for the process of programming, not for making efficient products. There has been no suggestion that educational software packages should be written in **Logo** (as they have in **Basic**). The **Logo** interpreter *is* the educational software package.

Procedural: Most modern programming languages, including the proposed standard **Basic**, are procedural, meaning that a program can be developed as a set of procedures. The procedure is the main conceptual device for tackling large programming problems, and for improving the readability and transferability of programs.

List-processing: **Logo** is essentially **Lisp** with a different syntax. Like **Lisp**, it provides commands for processing lists, which are data structures for representing information hierarchically. Unlike some other languages, it does not provide any other data structure (except numbers and strings).

Untyped: It is a matter of design philosophy whether or not to require a variable to be associated with a 'type', so that, for example, only integers may be assigned to a particular variable. An argument for types is that they discipline the programmer to use a variable for only one purpose: an argument against is that they are an unnecessary encumbrance in small programs. **Logo** has no types, but most other modern languages do. For example,

Algol68, one of the most elegant languages devised, makes the concept of type central.

Extensible: In **Logo** user-defined procedures can be used just like built-in procedures (unlike **Basic**). Almost all programming languages are extensible in this sense. In computer science, however, extensible usually implies a facility to add new types (as **Pascal** does, for example), new operators (as in **Algol68**), or new syntactic forms.[12] Only the last of these is provided in **Logo**, using a procedure to 'run' a list as a program. For example, in **Apple Logo**, a 'While' command can be added by defining

```
To While :Condition :Commands
   If Not Run :Condition [Stop]
   Run :Commands
   While :Condition :Commands
```

to be used as in, for example,

```
While [Heading < 90] [Forward 1 Left 1].
```

This is a little unsatisfactory because 'Run' is being used as both a command and a function (i.e. it may or may not return a result depending on its parameter) and because the syntax of new commands must use the list notation.

Logo's 'Run' is a legacy from **Lisp**, where the equivalent is an Eval function, which enables lists to be interpreted as programs (as noted earlier). However, **Logo** has introduced some problems in removing the round brackets that **Lisp** requires. For example, in **Apple Logo**, it is not possible to tell which of two consecutive procedure calls, A B, in a program is executed first without further information. This is because A could be a procedure requiring one parameter (in which case B would be evaluated first), or both could be procedures requiring no parameter (in which case A would be evaluated first). To resolve the problem it is necessary to look elsewhere in the program to see how A and B are defined. This may seem a minor technical quibble, but in fact the readability of a program is determined largely by how comprehensible small parts of the program are in isolation.

A solution in **Logo** is possible by insisting on a strict prefix form and by requiring two commands on the same line to be joined by an 'And'. Unfortunately, prefix form (e.g. 'Sum Product :B :B — (Product 4 :A :C)') is less acceptable to the **Logo** market than infix form (e.g. B×B — 4×A×C). Also, the round brackets in **Logo** are used around a procedure and its parameters, as in '(F :A :B)', not around the parameters alone, as in 'F(A,B)' in conventional mathematics. The colon in ':A' is necessary in **Logo** to indicate that the value of the variable A is required (not the name of the variable, which is denoted "A, nor a call of a procedure named A, which is denoted A). Thus, there are sound academic reasons for **Logo**'s use of prefix form and the special symbols [,], (,),: and ", but it is doubtful that **Logo** beginners appreciate them.

Some existing **Logo** implementations exhibit a certain amount of confusion in the use of quotes. Why, for example, in **Apple Logo** is a procedure definition written:

```
To Proc :Parameter
```

when

```
To "Proc "Parameter
```

would be more consistent with the other uses of " and :? In **380Z Logo**, one writes:

```
Build "Proc "Parameter
```

with the " before the Proc optional. This demonstrates another problem: the incompatibility between different implementations of **Logo**. There are arbitrarily different conventions for the names of primitives (To/Build, Value/Thing, Backward/Back, etc.), for the initial turtle direction (north/east), for dealing with hyphens (or minus signs) in lists, and so on. By the time this book is published, a committee to establish a **Logo** standard may well have been set up and we can look forward to it reporting in about 1994.

These kinds of consideration may appear to an educationalist to be unimportant technical detail. However, the realisation of philosophies such as those discussed in Chapter 10 depends upon the successful resolution of many such problems. The philosophies themselves may be promulgated largely independently of any particular programming language but it is naive to assume that these early versions of **Logo** will be adequate to carry out the programme proposed.

Now we must look at the recent and somewhat remarkable advocation of **Prolog** as a programming language for children. The focus is not on programming *per se* but on the virtues of logic. Logic 'for two thousand years has been one of the bases of our Western academic tradition'[13] and 'is the single academic discipline which is common to all subjects taught at school.'[14] In fact, logic is not, and never has been, a fundamental discipline. Even to the Greeks, logic (with grammar and rhetoric) was considered inferior to arithmetic which, with geometry, astronomy and music, made up the sterner disciplines. In any case, **Prolog** is based upon predicate logic, a system devised in the late nineteenth century and which bears little resemblance to the Greek variety. Perhaps **Logo** proponents should support their case by summoning up the academic heritage of geometry!

Prolog is a language for manipulating a database of propositions. A proposition consists of a predicate and some arguments, e.g.:

```
happy(fred)
kissed(fred,mary)
```

A statement in **Prolog** is either a question or a rule. For example:

```
happy(X)
```

is a question—in English, 'Who is happy?'—where the X is a variable which may be replaced by a constant. So if the database contained only the above two propositions then **Prolog** would respond:

```
X is fred
```

To see how **Prolog** works, let us first add two more propositions

```
happy(jack)
idle(jack)
```

and ask the question

```
happy(X),idle(X)
```

i.e. 'Who is happy and idle?' To answer this, **Prolog** first searches the database from top to bottom looking for a proposition that 'matches' happy(X). It finds happy(fred) and assigns 'fred' to X. It then searches for a proposition which matches idle(fred), which it does not find. It then automatically backtracks to find another happy(X). In this case, it will find happy(jack), and then idle(jack) and the question will be answered:

```
X is jack
```

In general, if **Prolog** reaches the end of the question then it effectively answers yes, and gives the values it has assigned to any variables; if it fails to find the required propositions it responds no. The key to **Prolog** is backtracking, but since this is automatic a programmer should, in principle, concentrate on the form of his question, not on how it is answered.

The other kind of **Prolog** statement, the rule, has the form:

```
proposition :- question
```

for example:

```
distraught(X) :- kissed(Y,X)
```

which might be rendered in English: 'To show that X is distraught show that X has been kissed by someone Y.' Or as a statement: 'Anyone kissed by someone is distraught.' These rules can also be added to the database and used to answer questions. If we asked:

```
distraught(X)
```

Prolog would use this rule, match 'kissed(Y,X)' with 'kissed(fred, mary)' and respond:

```
X is mary
```

(Of course, you will not be under any misapprehension that **Prolog** actually knows the meaning of 'happy', 'distraught' and so on.) In general, there might be several rules in the database with the same 'lefthand side', for example, there might be several ways of showing that someone is distraught. As before, **Prolog** will backtrack through the rules, if necessary, to find one that succeeds. The righthand side of a rule may itself be answered by using further rules, and so on. Clearly, for a database with a considerable number of propositions and rules, there may be much behind-the-scenes backtracking.

There has been much argument about the status of automatic backtracking. It can easily lead to excessively time-consuming searches. To provide the programmer with some control over backtracking, there is a 'cut' (written as an exclamation mark) which is used on the righthand sides of rules and prevents **Prolog** backtracking past that point, from 'right to left'. It is, however, difficult to make effective use of the cut. Hardy writes that

the precise meaning of some fragment of **Prolog** code can often be determined only by mentally simulating the actions of the **Prolog** interpreter on the code. Even then, the slightest misreading (such as ignoring a cut) will produce a widely inaccurate interpretation. . . . It is clear that although **Prolog** is powerful, it is hardly convenient. Frankly, it is an ergonomic disaster.[15]

But perhaps this is all irrelevant. Ennals[16] believes that 'it is likely that the new computer architectures will make backtracking obsolete.' This is a reference to the pre-emptive programme for 'fifth generation' computers, which has stimulated vigorous research into logic programming. In any case, he manages to avoid mentioning the cut at all in his book on **Prolog** for children.

For small databases and simple rules, the subtleties of **Prolog** can perhaps be ignored. Tallon, Ball and Tomley[17] describe how 13-year-olds can enter

```
organism(owls)
eat(owls,spiders)
carnivores(X)  :- eat(X,Y),animal(Y)
```

and so on, to build up their understanding of ecological systems. They point out the advantages for the pupil in building up the model himself, rather than having it hidden within a **Basic** program. While accepting this, I remain sceptical about the average child's ability to make sufficient sense of **Prolog** to gain much from such an exercise. According to Ennals:

Children progress easily from using interactive programs, to querying databases, and to writing their own programs. Their first simple programs will be written in their first week of a course. . . . It is easier for children, with their flexible minds, to learn logic programming than it is for veterans of conventional languages.[18]

These claims are beyond our experience with other languages (as described in Chapter 10) and the predictions of developmental psychology. Perhaps, as we noted before, 'programming' here means something less than it ought.

Particularly alarming is the claim that **Prolog** is 'based on human logic'. Whatever the benefits of the rigour of formal logic, it is not 'human'. As Wertheimer[19] remarked:

If one tries to describe processes of genuine thinking in terms of formal traditional logic, the result is often unsatisfactory; one has, then, a series of correct operations, but the sense of the process and what was vital, forceful, creative in it seems somehow to have evaporated in the formulations.

Not only is it unsatisfactory, it usually cannot be done at all. Much of what we would regard as common sense, involving purpose, cause and effect, process, and so on, could be represented in **Prolog**, if at all, only after deep research and with deeper opacity. Much philosophy of language this century has been devoted to the question of whether any form of predicate logic can express arbitrary English sentences that might appear in an argument. The evidence is against. Isolated formal reasoning is effective only with stark simplifications. Human reasoning depends on the prior setting-up of a system of precepts, complete with individual biases. (This is no 'proof' that computers cannot simulate human reasoning for they do not have to be programmed to follow the rules of formal logic.) It would be sad if teachers and their pupils believed that arguments which they could not express in the 'human logic' of **Prolog** were somehow inadequate.

The **Prolog** work has, however, had two welcome side-effects. First, it has demonstrated that both **Basic** and **Logo** have limitations for it would be difficult (especially in **Basic**) for pupils to carry out the kinds of exercises possible in **Prolog**. Secondly, it has shown that there are styles of programming different from that encouraged by both **Basic** and **Logo**. Programming in **Basic** and **Logo** is 'prescriptive', in that one prescribes how a result should be computed. Programming in **Prolog** is 'descriptive' since one describes the input/output relation to be satisfied. In principle, then, one is concerned with the correctness of the description not what the computer does with it.

13. Authoring Systems

None of the programming languages mentioned in the previous chapter was designed to be used to write educational software, although, of course, they may be used to do so, as we have seen. Rather than using general-purpose languages, however, an alternative is to try to design languages specially for writing educational software. As I mentioned in Chapter 12, programming languages tend to develop by generalising features that users seem to require. The biggest obstacle to developing special-purpose 'educational' languages is reaching some concensus on desirable features of such languages.

This emphasis on languages is misplaced, however, for the development of software depends more on extra-language facilities provided by the operating system environment in which programs are created, facilities, for example, to handle graphics, files, and so on. This environment, then, forms the 'authoring system'. An authoring system is a set of programs which helps a user (or 'author') to write educational software.

There are two main reasons why authoring systems have been developed. The first is the obvious one that it is cheaper to use tools appropriate to the job. Educational software of any quality is expensive to produce, and a high proportion of the cost lies in the design and implementation of the programs themselves. If some of this activity could be made automatic then the development time, and hence cost, would be significantly reduced. The second reason is that it might enable more teachers to be involved in producing educational software. Teachers, like anybody else, are reluctant to accept products thrust upon them—especially if these products do not accord with their own educational style and are, in any case, of inferior quality. Many teachers are tempted to write their own software. Many more, however, are deterred by the prospect of having to learn about programming. One of the aims of authoring systems is to enable teachers to write educational software 'without programming'.

However, the first authoring systems were presented as 'author languages', that is, as special-purpose programming languages designed to be usable by teachers untrained in programming. One of the first such languages was **Pilot**,[1] which has since been revived and is now available on many micros. Programs in **Pilot** are organised as a set of frames (as described in Chapter 9). A frame consists of presentation of text, diagrams and so on, followed by a pupil-response, after which decision rules determine the next frame to be presented. **Pilot** has a small repertoire of one-letter instructions (e.g. T, A, M, J, etc.) for performing standard operations (e.g. displaying text, accepting a student's response, matching a response with a specified word, jumping to a named frame, etc.). The most useful of these instructions are easily learned by the beginning author, so that small programs are soon written.

There is little evidence that the simplicity of author languages like **Pilot** helps teachers to write useful programs. In the United Kingdom there is very little **Pilot** software in genuine use. Denenberg,[2] writing with respect to the **Tutor** author language provided on PLATO,[3] considered that

while it is very easy for anyone to create a simple **Tutor** program in very little time, it is extremely difficult for anyone to write a moderately complex program using the structure afforded by the **Tutor** programming language. . . . The more useful lessons require a degree of expertise not commonly found even in many professional programmers.

Avner[4] found that it took teachers a full year to become competent in the **Tutor** language and that during this time they took little interest in pedagogical issues but 'became so involved in the use of [**Tutor**] that production of impressive sequences of animation or simulation became almost an end in itself.'

Part of the problem with author languages derives from the fact that they break almost all the rules in the programming language designer's book. They provide few control structures or data structures, emphasise labels and jumps, encourage cryptic notations, and so on. Here, for example, is a piece of **Staf**[5] which 'shows how a sequence of tests can be applied in order to select the routing, in this case to the next question of a quiz containing 26 questions':

```
#U10;O*  \$CLUBUB;$RNUBO6;$INUBO1;$EQSEO1;
         U15$DCUCUB;$GTUCOO;U55
         $INUCO6;U55*
#U15;O*  \$INUCUB;$NGUC26;U55$DCUC1O;U55*
#U55;O*  \$SWUC27;Z60V01V02......V26*
```

Staf was developed to 'provide teachers with tools with which to create their own teaching material' and 'to simplify the task of creating suitable programs'.

The first major authoring system, as opposed to author language, was provided with TICCIT.[6] The TICCIT designers believed that it was possible to separate course content from both computer programming and teaching strategy. Ideally, then, a teacher would be concerned only with the course content. The particular strategy embedded in **TICCIT** was based upon a rule–example–practice sequence, thought appropriate for concept learning. The author was relieved of the need to specify the detailed sequences of concepts by the provision of a 'learner control keyboard', using which the pupil was supposed to decide for himself which sequence to follow. However, since most pupils are not very proficient at determining their own strategies, **TICCIT** had also to support an 'advice button', which, to be effective, meant that **TICCIT** had to try to 'understand' what the pupil was doing and to have some notion of 'approved' sequences.

The idea of separating course content from the 'instructional logic' is important. If successful, it means that different content can be specified relatively easily. However, it does not necessarily mean that different logics can be provided for the same content: the logic is usually built into the system. The original TICCIT design, in fact, is not very good for specifying simulations and games, and subsequently a more conventional author language, **Tal**, has been provided to support these kinds of activities. The idea of separation also implies that different parts of the design process can be assigned to experts in different fields. Typically, TICCIT courseware, as educational software is called in the United States, is produced by a team including an instructional psychologist, a subject-matter expert, an instructional design technician, and a packaging specialist. Often the senior author (the subject-matter expert) has several assistant authors. Clearly, this team production of complex software brings the activity within the realm of software engineering, as discussed in Chapter 11.

In practice, **TICCIT** authors write educational software by filling in forms to describe the information needed to create a lesson. This is done either on paper or through a TICCIT terminal. There are several kinds of form, for example, one for processing answers, one for displaying text, and so on. These forms are then translated into a compact form for efficient processing when a pupil actually takes that lesson. With some authoring systems, an interactive program prompts authors to specify the information needed to generate the teaching programs. There are close analogies here with research on the interactive development of 'ordinary' programs.[7] The aim, of course, is to eliminate the need for an author to deal with the syntax or sequencing of author language commands, and so to give 'programmer-less creation of courseware'.[8] The incentive to claim that 'authoring' is not 'programming', so as not to frighten teachers, leads to a tendency to equate programming with coding and to dismiss the detailed specification and design of programs as not programming. (When discussing 'programming' by children we noted an opposite tendency, to count almost anything as programming.)

There are two further components of good authoring systems. First, there must be a sophisticated editor, for it must be easy to modify material in the light of classroom experience. These editors should help the creation and modification of graphics, but many are weak in this area. Secondly, authoring systems should support a 'course management function', that is, they should help the author manage the authoring process by, for example, providing ways to specify the data to be kept about subsequent student use of the material. The development of these two components is difficult, but not uniquely so to educational software.

Most developers of computer-based training material will make use of sophisticated authoring systems. For example, authors on WICAT computers use the **Wise** author language to 'compose text, design graphics, outline progress through courseware, and define criteria for evaluation . . . all without computer coding', and the **Smart** computer-managed instruction system 'to allow fully individualised training'.[9]

Apart from technical limitations, there are two main problems with authoring systems. The first derives from a conflict inherent in the design of any high-level programming system, that is, in the balance between easing the programmer's (or author's) task and in limiting what he can, in fact, do. Most authoring systems are best suited to the development of text-based, 'tutorial' lessons which follow a prespecified pattern. It is often difficult to specify, for example, the model needed for a simulation like **Newton** (Chapter 5). More generally, authoring systems, with their rigid frameworks, may stunt any teacher creativity.

The second problem lies with the pedagogical style fostered. Computer tutors are not 'personal Aristotles'. The 'frame-oriented' approach to developing educational software, in which bits of knowledge are packaged into chunks to be presented to students, does not lead to the detailed understanding by the computer tutor either of the material presented, or of the student's comprehension of it, which is necessary for a sophisticated tutorial. The mechanisation of regimented dialogues of the programmed learning variety (Chapter 6) is about the only area of computer-assisted learning where there is a sufficient concensus to enable authoring systems to be developed. No such concensus has yet emerged for the more creative, and perhaps more effective, modes of computer-assisted learning.

14. Designing Interactive Systems

Computer-assisted learning systems are members of the more general set of interactive systems. Much of the burgeoning research into the design of effective interactive systems applies directly to computer-assisted learning systems, although it has to be admitted that there are as yet few precise guidelines. The word 'system' indicates that we are concerned with more than the design of a single program. In principle, everything that influences how satifactorily a user interacts with a computer should be considered. This encompasses the fields of ergonomics, hardware design and human psychology, and so it will be necessary to limit ourselves to points particularly relevant to educational software.

This chapter is mainly concerned with the 'user interface', that is, with the means provided to enable a user to use a program: it is not concerned directly with whether the program is useful. We shall consider how easy it is for a user (teacher or pupil) to learn to use a program, not whether a pupil actually learns anything from the program, although obviously many of the same principles will apply. The word 'interface' should not be taken to refer just to physical objects, such as keyboards and colour monitors, for the most difficult problems are conceptual ones. They are concerned with what the user thinks of the system or, in the jargon, the 'user model'.

The first principle of interactive system design, then, is 'know the user'.[1] This immediately presents problems to CAL system designers, for there are two classes of user, teachers and pupils (three, if we count parents), of widely differing experience. For many other interactive systems, such as airline reservation systems, it is possible to assume, or even insist on, a certain level of competence, and this of course makes the design much easier. Moreover, few users of CAL programs will use them sufficiently frequently that they will routinely overlook the inevitable foibles and idiosyncracies, as regular users of other systems grow to do.

Most writers on the design of interactive systems present a list of guidelines (see, for example, Shneiderman[2]). These guidelines are not independent and, in fact, are often contradictory, and without a detailed investigation of how they influence actual system design they look little more than common sense. The vacuity prize, in fact, goes to a set of 'guidelines for educational software' produced by the Micro Users in Secondary Education group.[3] This suggests that 'information given to the user should be useful', 'the package should interact in an appropriate way', 'the package as a whole should be appealing to the user', 'error messages should be helpful', and so on. So, instead of presenting platitudes, I shall imagine a CAL system, **Strawman**, which appears to be badly designed in many respects. (Any resemblance to an actual system is entirely unfortunate.)

Some users find **Strawman** difficult to get started with. If **Strawman** is on tape, the cassette is usually misplaced. The cassette player is unreliable and it takes too long to load anyway. Before using the program there is some tiresome rigmarole to follow. When the user comes back to **Strawman** there is no easy way to continue from the point previously reached. Even if the user perseveres and become fluent with using **Strawman** there is no way he can abbreviate the initial greetings appropriate for beginners.

Assuming that the user manages to get **Strawman** running, he cannot find out what **Strawman** offers him, and so cannot judge whether he needs it. Unlike a book, where all that is on offer is at one's fingertips, most of a computer system is hidden. Users are frustrated by their inability to access what may be useful. Documentation would help, but for any non-trivial system it requires a substantial commitment of time for a potential user to read and learn how to use it. Teachers are too busy to learn how to use **Strawman** by trial and error, although some children will relish the chance to spend time on such puzzles whilst appearing to be doing something useful.

Users do not find **Strawman** easy to use because it is often unclear what is expected from them. Since the use of natural language is not feasible, even if it were thought desirable, all interactive systems require users to use an artificial language. The grammar of this language is often poorly defined and, in any case, may not be known to the user.

Various standard ways of carrying out man–computer dialogues have been devised. 'Menus', for example, are useful, particularly for novices. Options are displayed on the screen and the user picks the one he wants, either by typing the corresponding number, or by 'pointing' with a cursor or a hand-held device. This imposes few demands on the user's memory, assuming that he understands the options presented. However, with a complex program and several layers of menus, the experienced user will be annoyed by the time it takes to get something done.

'Command-driven' dialogues are more appropriate when the user wants to get directly to what he wants done, and when the job is a little more complicated to specify. A command may consist of a 'verb' followed by none or more 'objects' or 'arguments'. For example, 'print filename epson' may be a command to print a particular file on a printer. The user must know the form of the commands available. The definition of command languages, which are, after all, simple programming languages, is an established branch of computer science (see, for example, Unger[4] and Moran[5]).

The Computers in the Curriculum project has adopted a command-driven approach in most of its programs (although, for some unfathomable reason, the commands are called 'keywords', an already over-used term in computing). Their older style requires users to respecify all values (for a simulation like **Newton**, Chapter 5) even when they only want to change one.[6] (It does not follow that commands have to be adopted to overcome this limitation.) The members of the project believe that commands with arguments are 'bewildering to ordinary teachers and their pupils', and so the user is asked to specify the arguments separately.

Naturally, the words to identify commands are chosen to be meaningful (although some words, such as 'explain', may suggest more than they offer). Some will be specific to the particular topic, some (such as 'start', 'help', 'finish') may be common to many programs. Some commands may be so commonly used that it becomes tedious to type h, e, l, p, for example. So special keys may be provided, for example, TICCIT has a 'help' button, among others. This, of course, saves time and reduces typing errors. Many systems provide 'function keys' which do not have a pre-determined role, but can be given one by a programmer. For example, a music program may allow the user to use a function key to specify a crotchet, say. Many computer games, for example, **Space Invaders**, rely on the fact that a single key can be associated with a command, so enabling the user to get the maximum effect for the minimum input.

This trend towards using special keys and devices such as mice and paddles suggests that man–computer dialogues are becoming less, rather than more, like English dialogues. (A 'mouse' is a small box with wheels which is moved around a table top to drive a cursor on the screen.) The advantage of natural language for beginners, of course, is that most of them already know how to use it moderately well. Natural language, however, is verbose, vague and ambiguous, and if a system uses any natural language at all then a user may easily overestimate the system's language-understanding capabilities. Helping users to appreciate the extent to which computer dialogues are restricted is one of the hardest problems in interactive system design.

Perhaps the most important barrier for the educational software designer to overcome is that of subconsciously equating a screen with a page of text. The design of pleasing screen displays will be based on a completely different set of guidelines from those developed for graphics in books. The most important difference is that the display can be changed, but even the ground rules are different: blank space is now free, and so is colour (or almost so). We need new techniques for emphasis and for attracting attention. (I, for one, don't like being blinked and bleeped at.) Soon, I am sure, there will be a new breed of graphic designer employed routinely as a member of the educational software development team.

The specification of the 'user interface' presents great difficulties. The technique must be powerful enough to express interactive system behaviour with a minimum of complexity, and yet the specifications themselves must be easy to understand by both implementers, so that a correct system is produced, and users, so that they are not frustrated by not being able to work out what they are allowed to input. Most specifications have been based on one of two formal models: Backus–Naur form[7] and state transition diagrams.[8] The latter, perhaps, are more appropriate for processing the sequences of brief texts usual with interactive systems (rather than single long texts, such as programs). In a state transition diagram, such as that shown in Figure 14.1, nodes represent states, and lines between nodes have input/output events described on them. Figure 14.1 specifies a simple 'logging-in' sequence. For real interactive systems these diagrams can get very complicated, requiring as they do most of the paraphernalia of conventional programming languages, such as conditional commands, variables and procedures.

None the less, some such formal notation is essential to avoid confusion between designers, implementers and users of sophisticated interactive systems. The diagrams can be used not only to aid the development of procedures implementing the system but also to help users to understand the dialogue conventions. The problem is to ensure that users understand the notation. The ITMA project, which developed programs such as **Barset** and **Janeplus** mentioned in Chapter 6, has devised its own version of state transition diagrams (called 'drivecharts') for use by teachers when using their electronic blackboard programs. All ITMA programs are distributed with a 20-page guide to the use of drivecharts.

One of the benefits of using a 'standard' notation is that users become familiar with the consistent conventions. If we return to our hypothetical system, **Strawman**, it might be said to be inconsistent in several different ways. While many producers of educational software have developed standards or, at least, a style for their own programs, there is as yet little agreement on general conventions. The result is that teachers and pupils who use programs from different sources have constantly to re-adapt to a new set of conventions. This is particularly irksome for such users because they are unlikely to use programs sufficiently frequently that conventions become second nature. The inconsistency sometimes seems deliberately perverse: where one **Logo** editor uses F (to move the cursor forward), B (backward), P (previous line) and N (next line), another uses R (right), L (left), U (up) and D (down). To make matters worse, some of the letters mean something different in the other editor. An infrequent user of both editors has a frustrating time.

Until one convention is accepted as the 'best', there are bound to be inconsistencies between programs developed by different people, for much the same reasons that programming languages tend not to conform to standards. There is, however, less excuse

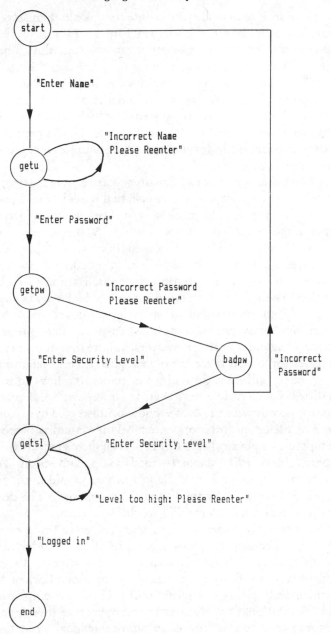

Figure 14.1

for programs which are not consistent with themselves. One editor uses a key to mean 'abort and forget what I've just typed' in one context, but the same key to mean 'stop and remember what I've just typed' in a second. Another program uses the 'esc' key to abort in one context but to continue in another. These sorts of inconsistency are fairly easy to avoid with small programs, but less so with larger interactive systems, which are collections of components developed by different people. Unless a specification is very precise, each developer will, to some extent, follow his own intuitions.

A more subtle form of inconsistency arises when a program or system conflicts with a user's 'conceptual model', that is, with the set of concepts which he already has or gradually acquires to explain the behaviour of the system. A simple example is a chemistry program which colour-codes its symbols, but does not use the colours which chemists have adopted.

More profound are those conceptualisations which users develop to help them understand a system which they have no wish or ability to understand at a technical level. For example, secretaries may understand a word-processing program by drawing analogies with typewriters. Where the program provides facilities for which there is no analogue (such as inserting blank lines), they will have difficulty understanding how to use those facilities. The need to ensure that, as far as possible, an interactive system accords with the user's model is illustrated by the design of the Star office information system.[9] This system is based on the metaphor of a physical office. The screen shows pictures of a desk, paper, folders, filing cabinets, mail boxes, and so on. To file a document you move it to a file just as you would in the physical world. ('Moving' is accomplished using a mouse.) The designers' aim is to make the 'electronic world' less alien.

Unfortunately, users of educational software bring or develop all kinds of conceptual models because of their widely different backgrounds and levels of expertise. To attempt to improve 'consistency' by developing analogues or metaphors of familiar learning and teaching activities will lead to a de-emphasis of the more revolutionary applications of computers. All designers seem to agree that consistency is an admirable goal even though it cannot be defined. Aldous Huxley once remarked that 'the only consistent people are dead people': perhaps the same applies to computer systems.

Another unquestioned, but undefinable, virtue is 'simplicity'. To criticise **Strawman** for being complex is to imply that it is *unnecessarily* complex. It may, for example, use arbitrary, and consequently easily forgotten, conventions. Or it may have avoidable technical restrictions. These complications may prevent users from forming the generalised rules which help users learn and remember how to use large systems.[10]

Our **Strawman** is also a program in which users easily get lost. It ensures this in several ways. If the user types something invalid (for example, a '6' when the options presented are 1–5) then **Strawman** does nothing but wait for a valid input. On the other hand, a valid input which initiates lengthy processing (for example, sorting a file) also provokes no response. The user cannot tell from the unchanged screen what is going on. At a higher level, **Strawman** provides no way for the user to find out where he is. It is not often appreciated how necessary this is. With a book, there are many clues which help readers know where they are, including the weight of pages on the left and right hands! Since computer programs do not follow an entirely predetermined sequence of activities, it is even more important to help users maintain their bearings within the structured activities they are carrying out. This, however, needs to be done with considerable tact if it is not to seem overbearing. As one example of what can be done, the TICCIT system included an 'adviser' program which students could use to find out where they were in a course and what they should do next.

This is a kind of 'help facility'. With educational software, help can be offered at two levels: either with how to use the system or with the content to be learned. The 'Help' command provided with Computers in the Curriculum programs is of the first kind. Users can ask for a brief explanation of what a command is for. This 'help' never varies and is not tailored in any way to the particular user. How much help should be available on-line rather than in accompanying documentation is a debateable issue. Few systems are able to respond adequately to direct pleas for help: even fewer are sufficiently omniscient to be able to offer help when it seems to be needed but is not requested.

Users will also criticise **Strawman** for being 'inflexible', meaning that they cannot 'bend' **Strawman** to serve their own needs. **Strawman** steamrollers all its users through the same routines. Providing alternative ways of expressing commands and adjusting the system to the user's experience can improve flexibility, but more generally it requires the developer to provide a wide range of options from which the user can select those he wants. On the other hand, users should not be bewildered by the profusion of options available. In general, the aim should be to increase the range of activities which can be carried out with the program and to increase the user's feeling of being in control.

One way in which systems can be made more flexible is by enabling the user to personalise the system by adding to the facilities available. A spelling program, for example, should allow users to put their own words in the dictionary. The Computers in the Curriculum programs usually allow users to rename the keywords and to sequence the options to provide a variety of predetermined pathways through the program. Similarly, on a larger scale, the Leeds teaching system (see Chapter 9) allows teachers to order the modules as they wish. These, however, are only selecting or re-ordering options already provided: few systems allow users to add new options because, of course, this would require programming expertise. Few programs can be easily modified except in minor ways. Few designers of educational software welcome users looking at, let alone changing, the program code: some make it impossible to do so.

Another reason why users should be able to modify programs easily is to enable them to overcome the deficiencies that soon become apparent. Our **Strawman** will be fragile (collapsing frequently), unreliable (running but giving inaccurate results) and unstable (failing if the user deviates slightly from the prescribed path). Of course, these bugs should not exist in the first place. But most of the changes a user might want to make are matters of taste: other users will no doubt want other changes. The point is that most users will not accept the apparently arbitrary aesthetics of someone else, especially when they know they should be easy to change. The designer's problem is to provide the user with something he wants and yet to leave him feeling that it is 'his' system.

Educational software is the first kind of resource that a teacher or a pupil should be able to adapt to his own needs. Books and films, for example, can be used in various ways but users cannot get 'inside' to change them. Teachers and pupils are the first body of users of computer software who, in the nature of their interests, will not be content to remain mere users: they will want to know how programs work and, knowing how, they will want to change them. This presents unique problems to the publishing industry. What, for example, happens about copyright? When does a modified program become a new program able to be published in its own right?

Even if publishers try to prevent users modifying programs, there is one aspect of 'maintenance' which should be provided, but rarely is. This is the facility to monitor the use of a program. We know very little about what users like, or dislike, about educational software and yet all programs are designed in a take-it-or-leave-it fashion. If a program provides, say, twenty options, why not design it to record how long users spend in those options? If a program asks questions, why not record how often the pupil answers correctly? These statistics may be of interest to teachers, but that is not their prime role: they are to help designers evaluate the usefulness of the programs they have developed. The complete absence of such monitors (which are common in other kinds of software) leads me to suspect that educational software designers would prefer not to know!

Finally, we must not leave our unhappy user still grappling with **Strawman**: we must help him stop. It is not possible to just type 'goodbye' and leave, and even if it were he would lose any files he is using. He must manoeuvre himself into some point at which he is allowed to stop and then follow some ritual almost as tiresome as the initiation ceremony.

To summarise, the designers of interactive systems in education face all of the problems common to the designers of other interactive systems,[11] plus a few more. In particular, there is an unusually heterogeneous body of users, who have a 'professional' interest in 'meddling' with the system. Since the use of such systems is a long way from being compulsory for teachers and pupils, it is especially important that they be sympathetically designed if they are to prove acceptable.

15.   Production Strategies

In this chapter we shall look at a variety of strategies which have been developed to produce educational software.

Much, perhaps even the majority, of the software in use in classrooms at the moment has been written by an individual teacher in his own time to serve his own purposes. This is inevitable given the shortage of good software from elsewhere and the desire of some teachers to educate themselves about what micros can do. Since the average teacher has neither the time nor the skill to write his own programs, most home-grown software is of the small-scale, worksheet variety.

Any teacher who does write his own software soon finds that his products and his expertise are in demand. For example, Houghton County Primary School, one of the first primary schools to get involved with micros, has sold software worth over £1000 to add to school funds to update their hardware. The writer of most of this software finds himself invited to discuss his work on television and is seconded to help produce the MEP Microprimer pack.

It often comes as a great surprise to software-writing teachers to discover that their hobby, which they might have vaguely hoped will produce something useful for their own pupils, leads to fame and fortune. While accumulating background material for the Open University Educational Software course, I wrote to about a hundred producers of educational software in Britain asking for up-to-date information about their products. Along with catalogues and leaflets, I received several letters explaining how particular organisations had developed. Many expressed surprise at their own success. The following is typical:

up to about two years ago, [I] had absolutely no experience of or with computers of any kind. I was lucky enough to be teaching in the same room that is used for computer studies at school and one day I started to experiment after a short demonstration by a colleague. I have always been keen on graphics and I wanted to see if it would be possible to use the computer to arrange the details of a drawing so that pupils could work more tidily. What started out as a vague idea has now developed into a most useful and versatile tool. I had no idea at the time that this sort of program would become a commercial proposition. However the program has become something of a small success with sales figures nudging 50 packages, and all on the strength of two new product reviews and a small mention in a software file.

This teacher has now set himself up as a registered company selling educational software.

The second main theme which emerged from all these letters was that producers were very critical of the quality of educational software products, at least those of producers other than themselves! For example, one teacher wrote that

It is my worry now there there will be a flood of poorly-written and educationally inferior products appearing soon . . . I only set up [my company] in the summer as a result of suffering overpriced and unstructured programs for so long.

Another letter deplored the fact that computer studies was 'abysmally badly taught by the average school teacher without sufficient experience' and extolled the virtues of programs written by a teacher after 'being at the receiving end of many, many moans from ill-taught students from schools and from ill-equipped teachers'. Another said:

I have read so many bad reports about programs, sadly many of them educational with dozens of bugs, poor screen displays, inadequate user notes and so on—that I was determined right from the start to offer a product that was ideally suited to the computer; educationally sound; as technically perfect as possible and with a practical and down to earth style.

So, many of the companies now advertising in the pages of educational magazines are the official face of an individual teacher who has discovered that he has a marketable product and is now striving, in his spare time, to produce good-quality educational software. He will find that he does not have the time to produce more than one or two programs a year, and even then he will skimp some stages, such as the thorough trialling in classrooms and the production of good user notes. He will not become a full-time educational software producer: there is not that much money to be made! He may, however, join forces with other teachers and experts in other areas in order to increase the volume and quality of his company's products. There are many ways this can be organised.

Netherhall School in Cambridge first became involved in educational software when they began supplying ideas to the Five Ways group and when some of their sixth-formers wrote programs for the Welcome tape provided with the BBC micro manufactured nearby. Some teachers at the school soon realised that this might prove a profitable independent enterprise. A group of teachers now develops ideas and writes specifications, which are then coded by an in-school programmer funded by the MEP. The MEP also helps to organise the trialling of the products, which are eventually published (with a subsidy from the MEP) by a commercial publisher. This is typical of the MEP's strategy of encouraging the grassroots development of educational software.

This progression had first been followed by Five Ways, who were the first school-based group to receive MEP support. Five Ways emerged from the King Edward VI School in Birmingham. In 1981–2 it received £132,000 from the MEP. By 1983 it had produced thirty packages, most selling for about £16 (again, this is an MEP-subsidised price). Five Ways had discovered that sixth-formers filling in a year between school and university are a fertile, but inexpensive, pool of programming talent. The directors of Five Ways believe that it is more important for these programmers to be enthusiastic and imaginative than that they should have any training in computing or education. Five Ways is now an independent company, seeking to expand its market into industrial training and looking for overseas sales.

The other two main recipients of MEP funds to develop educational software were the ITMA project at the College of St Mark and St John, Plymouth and the Computers in the Curriculum project, Chelsea College. The Chelsea group have been involved in the development of educational software since 1969, initially concentrating on secondary science simulations. These early programs were, according to Watson,[1] characterised by 'the active association with discovery-based learning' and were intended to encourage students to ask 'What would happen if . . .'. Clearly, there is a somewhat different notion of discovery learning here to that espoused by **Logo** enthusiasts, for example.

Today, the Computers in the Curriculum project has considerably widened its scope, so much so that Chelsea College now serves as a focus for a number of subject-based teacher groups which meet at different centres throughout the United Kingdom (e.g. a music group at Southampton, a languages group at Lancaster, and so on). These groups are intended to provide ideas for programs which meet the teachers' needs. The ideas are developed further by an author (a teacher) and a programmer working together. After reviews by the subject group, the programs and accompanying notes are tried out in a number of schools. After further revision in the light of the schools' comments, the programs are published commercially. This project, then, represents the most systematic approach in the United Kingdom to educational software development for schools. The productivity of the project is difficult to quantify: many of their products are reworkings of pre-micro programs, all of the programs run on some but not all micros, and there are always more programs 'in the pipeline'. In any case, a 'program' is a meaningless unit of productivity. It is clear, however, that the Computers in the Curriculum project is not producing packages as fast as the MEP directorate would like. This comment is no criticism on my part for, as I have indicated, the production of good educational software takes time and skill.

The ITMA project has also had some difficulty meeting the MEP's expectations, not least because the project sees itself mainly as a research group and only secondarily as an educational software developer. The members of the project are interested in investigating the use of micros as a teaching aid in classrooms. Their approach towards the development of educational software, described in detail in Burkhardt *et al.*,[2] differs from that of the Computers in the Curriculum project in two main respects. First, there is a greater openness in the very first step, that of coming up with an original, creative idea: Chelsea's committee-based approach is inclined to blunt individual initiative. Secondly, ITMA gives its programs a more thorough (some would say excessively thorough) try-out in classrooms. This is not only to evaluate the programs, but also to gather examples of how they might be used. These examples are then included in teachers' notes, to help other teachers. To some extent, the difference in approach reflects the fact that most of ITMA's programs are for the primary age-group, whereas most of Chelsea's are for the secondary level.

As this suggests, most groups developing educational software do not regard this activity as their only, or even their main, reason for existing: in addition to research, ITMA also runs in-service courses for teachers; the Computers in the Curriculum project is more interested in the curriculum than the computers.

There are many other groups which produce educational software as a by-product of their normal activities and without large external funding. One example is the SMILE centre in London. SMILE was set up in 1972 by the Inner London Education Authority as a scheme for individualised learning with mixed-ability classes in mathematics. One of its objectives is to provide as much variety as possible in the presentation of materials to children. The main resource is some 1400 work-cards, but there are also booklets, envelope packs, textbooks, wall-posters, audiotapes and television programmes. Recently, SMILE has begun developing microcomputer programs. Ideas are suggested by teachers, often during courses run by SMILE, and these are programmed by the teacher in his own time or by a programmer at the SMILE centre. The programs are advertised in the SMILE news journal as ready for trialling, and individual teachers volunteer to try them out. Once the programs are considered acceptable they are put in a 'library' and distributed free of charge to any teacher (within the ILEA district) who sends a disc. The programs are not consciously curriculum driven, are generally small, often poorly-written, with little documentation, and usually of the game variety. However, for a self-help group developing unpretentious educational software, the SMILE system seems a good model to follow.

All these organisations are essentially of teachers, i.e. of what one might have assumed to be buyers, not sellers, of educational software. The more conventional 'sellers' form a second class of educational software producer. Most micro manufacturers now advertise educational software in their catalogues to fill an otherwise conspicuous gap. Their lists are generally of products developed and distributed elsewhere, in particular by the teacher-based organisations mentioned above. The lists for the three

British government-approved micros remain thin: at the time the micros were approved, they were virtually empty (as discussed further in Chapter 20).

The leading United States micro companies (Apple, Atari, Commodore and Tandy) are able to provide much weightier catalogues of educational software, with an apparent policy of 'never mind the quality, include it in the catalogue'. Apple have developed a productive association with the Minnesota Educational Computing Consortium, probably the largest US government-funded educational computing project. In 1982, Apple tried (without success) to persuade the United States congress to let them 'give' a micro to all 80,000 schools in return for a 25 per cent tax credit. Atari, most associated with computer arcade games, have begun a multi-million dollar project in advanced educational applications, one of their aims being to store a comprehensive corpus of knowledge, such as the *Encyclopedia Brittanica*, so that a user can browse through it. In their scenario, 'browsing' involves a more or less guided tour of a computer-generated visual fantasy museum.[3]

Whilst micro manufacturers are relative newcomers to educational software, some mainframe computer companies have a long-standing involvement with computer-assisted learning. Control Data, for example, are still marketing the PLATO system developed in the early 1970s. One of the few examples of PLATO users in the United Kingdom is the Manpower Services Commission, which is using PLATO for a £1 million pilot project into computer-based training methods for disadvantaged youngsters. This amount of money is not easily come by in state schools, and so Control Data have developed a MicroPLATO system in which users use a stand-alone micro which can be linked to a mainframe to access PLATO lessons. In addition, Control Data are making some of their software available on other micros more commonly found in schools.

Other computer manufacturers have a wider interest in computer education. ICL, through their Computer Education in Schools team, have produced computer studies materials since the 1960s, and in 1982 began publishing case studies in the form of books supported by software available from MEP regional information centres. This team was transferred to Acorn Computers in 1983. The IBM subsidiary, Science Research Associates, now includes courseware (but not yet for the IBM personal computer) among its predominantly textbook-oriented materials. Many other textbook publishers have also begun to sell educational software (as discussed further in Chapter 16).

On the whole, however, most of the commercial enterprises in the production of educational materials have been content with advertising or distributing the products of others: they have not been too concerned with the actual design and development of the programs themselves. Another professional group, however, is becoming directly involved with writing educational software. These are the industrial training consultants, who have begun to look seriously at the potential advantages of computer-based training, for the reasons described in Chapter 6. For most, the use of computers is still an experimental supplement to their established procedures of intensive lecture courses based on detailed manuals. Others, who might be associated with a particular computer manufacturer, will work exclusively in computer-based training. For example, WICAT are actively supporting the development of industrial training systems for their 68000 range of micros, which are more powerful than any of the micros found in state schools. One such system is being used by British Telecom through their network of training centres.

These projects are characterised by a realistic commercial approach quite unlike that of educational software developers for schools. In particular, they will have a more professional attitude to software development. The levels of funding involved are so different as to ensure that there is little cross-fertilisation of ideas. Even allowing for the fact that students in industrial training have different motivations from those at school, I am sure developers of software for schools would benefit from studying the work being done in computer-based training.

16.   Publishing

This short chapter considers the final stage of educational software production. Turning a useful program into a marketable product requires a different set of skills and experience, and it is natural to turn to established commercial publishers to provide them. These publishers have their own reasons for wishing to sell educational software. It is well recognised that selling educational software is a more complicated activity than selling textbooks, but it seems to be benignly assumed that publishers will be able to overcome the problems. My own feeling, however, is that the solutions that will be devised will be harmful to the quality of educational software products.

The 'educational software industry' has barely begun, and it is futile to try to predict its eventual form, but let us look at some likely developments over the next few years.

1. Higher prices will be charged.

At the moment, products for schools in the United Kingdom are subsidised by the MEP, produced by hobbyists for whom any income is a bonus, or competing with these. Prices are therefore artificially low, although teachers regard them as high. When realistic prices are charged—and outside education and the computer games market almost no software can be bought for less than £50—only the most well-endowed (and least needy) schools will be able to afford them. Alternatively, prices will be held at the present level, either by perpetual subsidies or by a decrease in the quality of educational software products, if such a thing be possible.

2. Educational software will be distributed as a 'multi-media package'.

Recognising the ease with which programs can be copied illegally, publishers will ensure that programs form only part of a learning package. According to Johnstone,[1] 'documentation can be kept to one sheet per program' and 'it seems peculiarly perverse to write a computer program which depends for its actual ease of use on a piece of paper.' Actually, any program worth writing requires considerable user documentation—for example, **Visicalc**, the best-selling micro program of any kind, is distributed with a 90-page manual. The potential harm lies not in the inclusion of superfluous documentation but in the temptation to make programs unnecessarily incomprehensible and difficult to use on their own.

3. Alternatively, programs will be distributed in an unreadable and uncopyable form.

This technical solution (at present unfeasible) to illegal copying would compel teachers and pupils to accept, or reject, programs in exactly the form in which they are distributed. It would not be possible to adapt programs for individual needs.

4. Publishers will turn to the home, rather than the school, market.

Unless programs are made uncopyable, schools will not buy more than one copy of a program, as they do textbooks, and so there is a limited market for educational software products. There are more micros in homes than in schools and products can be sold to home users on an individual basis. Inevitably, therefore, publishers will direct their efforts to home users. At the moment, most publishers are concentrating on schools because they have established procedures for the school market and because they feel, with justification, that present products are unsuitable for home use. Some commentators welcome the prospect of substantial learning taking place in the home through the new information technology, seeing this as initiating a revolution in the state educational system. This shows a touching faith in the ability of designers to produce good-quality educational software for the home user, and in the ability of members of the public to recognise, and buy, good-quality products. A more likely outcome, given that the average home user has less money and a less powerful computer than the school user, is an even greater emphasis on the cheap and glossy drill-cum-game. One of the first educational publishers to aim for the home market promises us 'a typical "unit", selling at £5–£10, [which] will be a pack of one or two cassettes or disks, containing, say, half a dozen programs on number work for junior school children, plus a workbook of related and unrelated exercises.'[2] What kind of a program can we expect for a few pence?

5. Publishers will standardise products.

In order to maximise sales and minimise costs, publishers will impose standards on the programs they publish. The aim will be to ensure that programs can be transferred as easily as possible to other micros and changed easily when micros are upgraded, and also to ensure that accompanying documentation does not have to be rewritten for different versions. This makes good commercial and technical sense, although, as usual in educational computing, the work will be attempted ignoring computer science research on standardisation[3] and portability.[4] However, the effect will be, as with all premature standardisations, to ossify products at the level of the lowest common denominator since, in the interests of compatibility, the more advanced features of some languages and computers will be eschewed. An equally worrying prospect is that curriculum development itself will be restrained. This may seem paradoxical for there is now a burst of activity in trying to redesign the curriculum to take account of the new technology. However, the strategy of most educational software developers is to pick off, piecemeal fashion, topics from the conventional curriculum. So, for example, the mere existence of a well-known program called **Climate** will ensure that no one else will write a climatology program for several years: why face competition when there is so much virgin territory?

6. Publishers will influence the kinds of programs written.

It is a mistake to see commercial publishers as passive intermediaries between author and reader. They may appear so in the textbook field because there publishers and authors are generally agreed on aims and markets, dictated by present curricula and examinations. Publishers of educational software are bound to prefer safe, curriculum-based products for which they perceive a market: innovation is a risky investment. Publishers, in their eagerness to cover the field first, may well commission programs for particular topics.

It is clear that many publishers are embarking on educational software products in order to keep a watching brief on developments rather than from any conviction that profits will ensue. Most are uneasy at the new technical complications, such as telesoftware and videodisks. Most, too, dislike the fact that producers almost invariably deliver programs late and with bugs, for which the publisher then gets blamed. Educational computing enthusiasts are so in step with the march of progress that it seems inevitable to them that publishers will rush to market their products. I suspect, however, that within the next five years many publishers will withdraw from educational software, deciding that the profits, if any, are not worth the problems.

PART 4

Problems with Educational Software

In Parts 2 and 3 we looked at the variety of functions which educational software might fulfil and considered how educational software might be produced. There is much to criticise and to question, and it may seem unfair to be so critical of efforts to overcome the inevitable teething problems: surely there will soon be a plentiful supply of good quality software? Alas, the problems are more deep-rooted, and after twenty years designing educational software we can hardly continue to describe them as 'teething problems'. I believe that much that is being done today will never lead to solutions to these problems. If computers are to be used in education on the scale being encouraged, we owe it to coming generations of pupils to think carefully about the software we provide for them to use.

17. The Philosophy of Educational Computing

Philosophers of education justify the existence of what is called 'education' in essentially two ways: in terms of the needs of the individual, and in terms of the needs of society. Advocates of educational computing use the same two arguments. If it is our ethical and moral responsibility to educate pupils in order to help them to live more interesting and intrinsically worthwhile lives, and if computers can, in fact, enchance this educative process, then clearly computers should be used in education. Likewise, if it is in the public interest to improve the general level of understanding of computers (if only to improve the economic well-being of the community), then again computers should be used. The first kind of justification leads to the advocation of computer-assisted learning, the second to proposals for 'computer awareness' or 'computer literacy' courses (which we shall discuss briefly in Chapter 20).

In the broad sense, education is concerned with the transmission of humane values such as compassion, integrity and justice, but few would claim that computers are likely to be of much help here. More narrowly, education is concerned with the development of knowledge and understanding. What, then, is the nature of knowledge, and how can computers help in its acquisition? Educational philosophers have always implicitly assumed that certain kinds of knowledge are more worthy than others. Plato, for example, emphasised mathematical knowledge on the grounds that this knowledge is at least certain whereas other kinds of knowledge are mere opinion (according to Plato). Dewey considered scientific knowledge most worthwhile since it enables us to control the quality of our lives. Today, we see the beginning of a philosophy that the only worthwhile knowledge is the computational, on the grounds that if we cannot program it we do not possess it.

To say that knowledge is of a certain kind is not to say that knowledge belongs to a certain class, say, within a certain part of the curriculum: it is to say that the knowledge can be expressed in a certain form. So, for example, knowledge of music could be considered 'mathematical' knowledge if it could be expressed in mathematical form, that is, using ordinary mathematical notations and concepts. It could also be considered 'computational' knowledge if it could be expressed in computational form, that is, as a computer program. So, the role of computers in education rests fundamentally on what is 'programmable'. It is not possible at this stage to say precisely where the limits lie. It is possible to say, however, that there *are* limits, for it is known formally that there are some problems which cannot be solved by computer. More practically, we can say that the difficulty of representing many kinds of knowledge as computer programs will ensure that, for many years at least, most educational software will possess only the most superficial knowledge. Even if, in due course, we find that all worthwhile knowledge is indeed programmable it does not follow that it will be represented in educational software, for there is no guarantee (in fact, it seems quite implausible) that such programs will be practically useful: they are very likely to be exorbitantly expensive to write and to run.

It is worth remembering that all educational philosophies are tied to a social and political context: it seems impossible to judge philosophies in the abstract, as it were. Plato's proposal that the educational system should aim to produce just men by developing their fundamental differences was partly intended to re-establish the Athenian aristocratic élite which was being overthrown by the Spartans. Rousseau's contribution to educational theory, which emphasised the role of free exploration by children for the development of mature citizens, helped to establish the intellectual climate through which the French Revolution could bring about a modern-style democracy.

Like Rousseau, Dewey also emphasised a child-centred philosophy, but with the tacit aim of developing resourceful artisans for the urban democracies of the early twentieth century. Today, there is a general perception that a technology-based revolution is underway changing the form of society. Naturally, modern philosophies of education are oriented towards producing people able to live productively in some hazily perceived technological society of the future. Indeed, an educational policy which seeks primarily to promote prosperity through technological development is hardly a philosophy of education at all.

It is recognised (as it has always been in educational philosophies) that the *content* of knowledge is much less important than higher-level skills, such as knowing how to reason about knowledge, how to acquire new knowledge, how to adapt to it, and so on. With the increasing pace of change such skills are even more crucial. Now the focus is more on the activity of learning than the result. How do computers affect this activity?

Education, more than any other profession such as law or medicine, has depended upon sympathetic communication between individuals in order to achieve human goals. Almost by definition, it seems dehumanising to automate any part of this activity. Of course, this comment is more valid for some software than others. But any software requires its users to interact with it in an artificial or, as Mumford[1] neatly put it, 'denatured' language: 'something essential to man's creativity, even in science, may disappear when the defiantly metaphoric language of poetry gives way completely to the denatured language of the computer.' I am not too concerned about the patently unnatural programming languages because any user of **Basic**, **Logo** and their successors knows that he is engaging in an activity for which a special language may be necessary, as it is for, say, knitting and composing. But what about the more routine uses of computers (think back, for example, to the interactions with **Climate**, **Adventure**, **Factfile** and others)? As we know, children have a remarkable ability to develop a mastery of their natural language. How will this be affected if, as many prophets foresee, children spend several hours a day communicating with computers? The average child today already spends more hours watching television that he does attending school and no doubt much of this will transfer to computers. Will it matter if children spend long hours typing only one-key answers or using only two-word imperatives (without even the normal conventions of politeness!)?

Education is also a social event, not just because some activities require more than one participant but also because social skills have to be learned. Educational software designers need to think much more carefully about the social environment in which their programs will be used. Amarel[2] argues that the effect of computers on the social organisation of classrooms will be a greater determinant of educational outcomes than the content of the software itself. One group admits to designing programs for the day (which they see as imminent) when many schools will have rooms full of individualised computer booths. At the other extreme, some designer's believe that time spent using programs should be minimised because learning occurs more through class discussion stimulated by the program. Outside schools, will children really use educational software, probably in isolation, at home? If so, is this socially desirable? It is surely too optimistic to hope that 'the need to come together for such things as practical/laboratory work or sports events and fixtures could look after [the social aspects of learning].'[3]

Some of the most difficult philosophical questions centre on the issue of whether computers can and ought to teach. Strictly, of course, no machine can teach because it has no intentions (as discussed in Chapter 2). It is the 'computer plus software' which must be considered the teaching agent, for the software certainly does carry intentions. Programmed computers display such astonishing capabilities that we naturally expect much more:

Within the very near future—much less than twenty-five years—we shall have the technical capability of substituting machines for any and all human functions in organizations. Within the same period, we shall have acquired an extensive and empirically tested theory of human cognitive processes and their interactions with human emotions, attitudes, and values.[4]

This prediction, by one of America's most influential scientists, that computers will be able to teach, among many other things, was made in 1960.

Alongside the inevitability of technological 'progress' runs the psychologist's conviction (unspoken since the behaviourists' unfulfilled claims for teaching machines) that, as they discover more of the nature of human learning, so teaching will become more an explicit technology. Hence, according to one philosopher, writing in 1967, 'it was inevitable that machines would occupy a central place in the classroom.'[5] The fallacy here, however, lies in the assumption that what psychologists discover must, *ipso facto*, be 'computational knowledge', that is, knowledge which can be expressed as computer programs.

The belief that computers can, in principle, do anything humans can do—and much more besides—naturally provokes discussion. The most trenchant criticism of this belief has been made by Weizenbaum,[6] who writes:

the human is unique by virtue of the fact that he must necessarily confront problems that arise from his unique biological and emotional needs. . . . No other organism, and certainly no computer, can be made to confront genuine human problems in human terms.

But, to Weizenbaum, the issue is not what computers *can* do but what they *ought* to do. He describes two kinds of computer applications that, in his opinion, ought not to be undertaken: first, those projects 'that propose to substitute a computer system for a human function that involves interpersonal respect, understanding, and love', and, secondly, those 'which can easily be seen to have irreversible and not entirely foreseeable side-effects [and which] cannot be shown to meet a pressing human need that cannot readily be met in any other way.'

In neither case does he proscribe educational applications of computers (he actually cites computerised psychotherapy and automatic speech recognition), but it seems to me that such applications might well qualify on both counts. In an increasingly automated world, is it inevitable, or even desirable, that children should be encouraged to learn from impersonal machines which, as we have seen, have no significant understanding? Is a responsive human relationship essential for real learning to take place? Is there any harm in children increasingly fantasising within charlatan microworlds? What human values will children develop from using programs which, in a few hundred lines of **Basic**, purport to understand what determines a politician's popularity? How does the hard, macho computer image affect the intuitive aesthete? In a society which already suffers from an over-emphasis on the rational (i.e. logical, computable), is it sensible to encourage this mode of thought even further? What 'pressing human need' are micros in schools fulfilling, remembering that government money could have been spent on employing and retraining human teachers instead? It is, however, against the spirit of the age to question the possible social and cultural consequences of using computers in education.

18.   The Misdirection of Enthusiasm

The introduction of computers to education is being led by a remarkably dedicated and hard-working band of enthusiasts. Many of them, in addition to carrying on normal teaching duties, voluntarily run courses for the uncommitted, work through the night writing software to meet unrealistic self-imposed deadlines, and offer their new-found expertise to anyone prepared to listen. A few occasionally find the time to commit their enthusiasm to print. Here are some samples:

> What is it about **Space Invaders** which gives it its Pied Piper quality? If we can identify this and harness it to the furtherance of educational ends the thirst for education could spread like an epidemic. Not merely the thirst; the attainment too . . . if the right sort of software can be created on a comprehensive enough scale the common educational stature of the human race could go soaring.[1]

> The microcomputer . . . now seems likely to revolutionise the whole environment of learning worldwide.[2]

> The future is full of opportunity for imaginative teachers to use the new technology to complement existing skills and give new life to the term 'curriculum development'.[3]

What is the reason for such enthusiasm? It would be nice to believe that it results from an objective assessment of what has already been achieved in educational computing. Of course, it does not, for most evaluations have been unconvincing. In any case there are real problems in carrying out evaluations (as discussed further in Chapter 19).

Perhaps there is a more practical reason for enthusiasm. When a bandwagon rolls, it is better to be on it than under it. In an underpaid and contracting profession, it does not take much perception to see that one of the few areas for personal advancement is in the computing field. There is a shortage of trained computing teachers and, outside teaching, there is a variety of jobs (computing adviser, magazine editor, itinerant lecturer, etc.) which can be taken on, part-time or full-time. Most of the first generation of enthusiasts are no longer teachers because, of course, the computationally skilled can seek more lucrative employment outside teaching.

What sort of teacher is it that takes up the computing banner? In the first place, no doubt, it is the teacher who sees it as his professional duty to become familiar with the new technology so that he can convey his understanding to his pupils. He will begin by writing programs and may discover, much to his surprise, that he has an unsuspected talent for doing so. Much has been written on the compulsive seductiveness of computer programming, especially for beginners. It occurs with pupils of all ages, including teachers. The compulsion arises essentially from the delight in mastering worlds of one's own creation and the gratifying appearance of success in learning a highly-prized technical skill. In reality, our teacher has only reached the first plateau of a mountain range, but it is sufficient to convince him that he has found his true vocation. Henceforth, he will become one of a new breed, a teacher-cum-programmer (or tcp, for short).

The wave of micros in education is riding on a small band of self-selecting tcps, unrepresentative of teachers as a whole. Good teachers do not necessarily have the kind of mentality—an introspective fussiness, perhaps—which enjoys programming. What is clear is that the enthusiasm of tcps does not derive entirely from a cool analysis of the needs of pupils but in part from their own position as computer 'experts'.

It is commonly believed that enthusiastic teacher involvement is the key to overcoming resistance to technological innovation in education, and that assigning a group of outside 'professionals' to develop new materials for schools is bound to fail. (This, of course, is only relevant to situations where teachers hold the reins of control; it does not apply to learning at home, for example.) If this belief is correct, then aren't the enthusiasts to be wholly welcomed? It depends on whether one approves of the enthusiasts' aims.

Tcps do not begin with a commitment to an educational philosophy which they wish to implement, nor with a deep understanding of the capabilities of computer technology. Having learnt to write simple programs, their first problem is finding they have nothing to write programs about. The producers of the MEP Microprimer pack, began with a general appeal for ideas for software, offering the princely sum of £100–£200 for detailed specifications. Two decades earlier, in a different context, the lesson had been learnt, but now apparently forgotten:

Many programmers realized that they had been programming things that should never have been taught at all, or that should have been taught by some other method or combination of methods. More and more they saw the folly of setting out with a medium in search of a message. They began to concentrate on deciding first what might be learned (the message) before deciding how it should be taught (the medium).[4]

The programmers' referred to here were not computer programmers but the authors of programmed learning material.

With no deep knowledge to guide their enthusiasm, tcps remain convinced that the real 'stuff' of educational computing lies in the day-to-day trivia of micro trappings and the 'frontier research' being done by real teachers in real classrooms. The educational computing enthusiast so busies himself that he has insufficient time to think much about what he is doing and to keep up with new developments. I find it alarming, for example, that one of the MEP's national coordinators can write (while commenting on a draft of our Open University course, which mentioned the programming language **Smalltalk**): 'I have never heard of **Smalltalk**, is it likely to emerge from a small number of universities? Or will it disappear into the void where so many languages have been consigned?' The **Smalltalk** language and operating system has been under development since about 1970 and it has been clear for many years that it introduced concepts which would influence future computer system design. Within a few weeks of the above remark, a prominent editorial commented that

software companies appear to be staking their future on products that feature video windows, which allow various projects to appear on the video screen simultaneously, and the mouse, a hand-held box-shaped device that provides an alternative to the computer keyboard.[5]

Both windows and mice were pioneered by **Smalltalk**. Ignorance is forgivable when there is so much of relevance to understand, but not the bland assumption that nothing of relevance to educational computing occurs outside the school classroom.

A rare insight into the tcps' *modus operandi* in developing educational software is given by Smith,[6] who describes the many iterations involved in producing **Spell**, a program to help with primary children's spelling. Normally, we only see the final product. Here, in summary, are the successive versions of **Spell**:

1. The program repeatedly drew a word (selected at random from data) in large, lower-case letters, with one letter (selected at random) missing. A number was displayed, referring to a sheet of pictorial clues. The child had to type the missing letter. The teacher could change the words in the data.

2. 'The next stage was to consider the program as just one aspect of an overall approach to teaching and reinforcing spelling.' So three options were provided: one to specify in the data the position of the missing letter, the second to allow for the omission of two or more consecutive letters, and the third to show the entire word only briefly.

3. Now the teacher, not the child, selected the options.

4. A default option was provided.

5. The words were grouped in 'levels' (e.g. initial blends, vowel digraphs, etc.), the teacher selecting an appropriate level.

6. The pupil was allowed to delete a typed letter.

7. The random selection of words was modified to select each word once only.

8. The letter-drawing routine was changed to draw letters in the way children are supposed to write them.

9. A word could be made to reappear by typing a question mark.

10. Since the program now needed rewriting for a smaller micro, the various options (which teachers did not like, anyway) were dispensed with, and the one program became two or more separate programs.

11. The levels, which 'dictated a phonic approach to reinforcing spelling', were also dispensed with. Teachers again had to type their own words as data.

12. A separate program was written to help teachers create their datafiles.

And so, no doubt, it goes on. The conclusion drawn is 'that this case study has shown the degree of involvement and communication that is necessary to produce a reasonably good educational program.'

My conclusions are rather different. There must be a better way to write educational software than by laborious tinkering. To start with, we must *begin* with a better idea of what we want to achieve, not leave it to 'the next stage'. We must also be prepared to learn from others: nowhere in Smith's paper is there any suggestion that work carried out elsewhere had influenced the design. The interface problems with **Spell** could surely have been anticipated by anyone familiar with interactive systems design. In addition, it is hard to believe that there is nothing of relevance in the volumes written by educational psychologists on reading and spelling. Even within computer-assisted learning, there have been spelling programs since at least 1965.[7] Programmers of all kinds are notorious for not reading the literature: somehow a deep understanding is supposed to materialise from the succession of patches to overcome 'temporary' difficulties.

The tcp is dismissive of 'research whose maximum possible achievement will be establishing some morsel of fact which every seasoned school teacher knows perfectly well already.'[8] He believes in 'real teachers who are doing the real innovating with real pupils.' The tcp is particularly scornful of the 'programmer', a term of abuse directed to the hypothetical individual writing educational software in ignorance of good educational practice. It is hard for teachers to believe that present educational software could possibly have been written by other teachers. The fact is that there are very few, if any, professional programmers (in the sense that the job description would be understood in the software industry) writing educational software—at least, not for schools. The reason is obvious: they would be much more gainfully employed writing other kinds of software.

It is understandable for practising teachers to be unsympathetic to contributions from 'experts' outside the educational ranks, but it is sad that the myth that programmers are to blame for the poor quality of educational software has led to a rejection of anything associated with 'computer science'. Chandler[9] finds it advisable to reassure readers in his very first sentence that he is not a computer scientist. Black[10] considers that the most important question to consider when evaluating software is 'has it been researched, written and evaluated by teachers?' Publishers think it wise to emphasise that their programs are written by teachers. Why are teachers, alone of the professions, so insistent that only they are able to write software to meet their needs? Lawyers and doctors, for example, do not expect to write programs, although of course some of them must be involved in the programs' design. Could it be that teachers are sensitive to the revelation that they do not know precisely what they are trying to do or how they do it? The fragile professional status of teachers would crumble further if they were to accept 'external' dictates concerning educational practices.

The tcp comes then (after eliminating as irrelevant all of computer science, educational psychology, curriculum design, and much more) to the delusion that he has mastered a difficult craft and so feels qualified to dispense his wisdom. Consequently, tutorial articles in educational magazines are riddled with technical mistakes and misconceptions. Here is just one example from any number:

for those of you who do not know, **Pascal** combines the features of **Basic** and **Fortran** producing a high-level language which it is fairly easy to get started with.[11]

In addition, the tcp can, from his platform of new-found expertise, pontificate on matters on which a few months earlier he would not have presumed to offer an opinion. He will not hesitate, for example, to make far-reaching proposals for curriculum change.

In the face of this awesome authority and expertise, the teacher new to computer technology may be inclined to accept that computers are inquestionably a 'good thing'. To those who express doubts, the tcp has an 'emperor's clothes' argument: 'it is your own lack of imagination which stops you seeing the potential.'[12] That the tcp's own head-down enthusiasm could also lead to an impairment of the visual faculties seems not to have occurred to him.

19. The Institutionalisation of Mediocrity

This chapter addresses two questions: first, what is the quality of present educational software?, and second, what are the prospects for better quality software in the future?

No disinterested observer will be surprised by the opinion expressed here that most educational software is of poor quality. Many others have come to the same conclusion:

there is widespread agreement that the state of the art of educational software development leaves much to be desired;[1]

much of it is poorly programmed and/or pedagogically inadequate;[2]

critics of new information technology point out, with some justice, that the courseware available so far for use in the new machines is inadequate in quality, quantity and variety;[3]

a mountain of poor-quality educational software seems to be accumulating with only a molehill of quality.[4]

Perhaps we should ignore the lamentable state of present software and ask instead whether we are now in a better position to write good quality software.

First, however, we should consider how one arrives at a judgement of the quality of educational software. Are the above opinions simply subjective impressions or are they based on some kind of empirical evidence? If they are subjective, they may easily be countered by equally subjective enthusiasm. For example, some of the Microprimer programs (of which more later) are described as 'truly excellent',[5] admittedly by one of the authors. The castle-building tcp will, in fact, detect many signs that his products are of high quality. First, sales are good—but present levels of sales are determined by the compelling need of educationalists to justify the time and money already spent on introducing computers into education. In any case, quite respectable sales can be notched up by selling only to the numerous advisory centres set up partly to enable teachers to sample software before buying. Secondly, many teachers seem happy with the products. The teachers that tcps encounter are mostly volunteers for teacher-training update courses. These teachers are necessarily a small, enthusiastic subset of all teachers. The average teacher is inclined to believe that there simply *must* be good software to justify the enforced revolution. It may be offensive to say so, but teachers do not necessarily possess all the skills needed to form a proper judgement. Lastly, pupils like using the programs. This is the most beguiling fact about present software. It might be thought a desirable, even necessary, condition to be met by good quality educational software that pupils find it enjoyable to use, but it is not a sufficient condition. In short, we must reject 'market forces' as a judgement of quality, and ask bluntly, do computers aid cost-effective learning?

There are two aims of evaluation: to provide decision-makers with information about the effectiveness of an educational programme or product, and to provide evidence for modifying a programme or product to improve the pupils' learning. Many different and detailed models for carrying out evaluations have been proposed (see Borich and Jemelka[6] for a summary). At one extreme, we can distinguish a view of evaluation as simply 'professional judgement'; at the other, evaluation involves the accumulation of data concerning whether performance meets objectives. The former is, of course, much easier in principle to carry out since it only requires an expert to consider whatever qualitative and quantitative variables he thinks are appropriate to arrive at an opinion. But the objectivity and reliability of the judgements are always questionable. The latter view of evaluation, on the other hand, forces educators to define measurable objectives which can form criteria for judging effectiveness. Naturally, this leads to a neglect of objectives which cannot be easily measured.

Within computer-assisted learning, the issue of evaluation seems to have been shelved. Almost all evaluation, if it deserves the term, is of the subjective 'professional judgement' variety. This is partly because it is particulary difficult to specify objectives when computers are themselves causing 'traditional' objectives to be questioned. In addition, lengthy, controlled experiments cannot easily be carried out in such a rapidly evolving situation. I also suspect that there is a legacy from the computer-assisted learning evaluations carried out in the 1970s. The large-scale PLATO and TICCIT projects in the United States suffered formal evaluations which produced inconclusive verdicts. Similarly, the more impressionistic evaluation of the Brookline **Logo** project (see Chapter 10) did little to convince the sceptics. The conclusion drawn has not been that computer-assisted learning does not work, but that the evaluation of computer-assisted learning does not.

It was the March 1983 edition of the *Educational Computing* magazine which persuaded me that my disillusionment with educational software was not ungrounded and that it was not premature to criticise. The magazine had reviews of three educational software packages. One, **Early Learning**, contained five programs: three arithmetic drills (two of which had already been widely distributed); a program in which Billy Bulldozer shunts words around the screen with the aim of teaching the effect of putting an 'e' at the end of a simple word or letter group; and a variation of 'Hangman' in which Jumbo misses out on a drink if the word is not completed. The reviewer considered this 'one of the best commercial educational software packages to date'.

The second, **Superhangman**, used 'extremely good' graphics, 'right down to the blinking eyes', and used a fanfare or dirge to mark success or failure. This was judged 'definitely one of the best spelling programs for the BBC machine'.

The third package included **Bomber** (mentioned in Chapter 8), **Numbervaders**, **Four-in-a-Row** and **Shootout**, the last three being based on **Bomber**. This was rated 'a genuine attempt, by a teacher, to provide a quality piece of software . . . the idea is very good.' In addition, the magazine contained a review of a book about Bigtrak, a tank which can be programmed (provided programming is equated with button-pushing, see Chapter 10), and an advertisement for **Logo Challenge**.[7] According to one reviewer of **Logo Challenge**,[8] 'the whole package is very professional' and represents 'a great advance in our resources'.

Logo Challenge enables children to define procedures to draw pictures. One of the many faults in the implementation is that a procedure is executed at the same time as it is defined so that, for example, while a House procedure is being defined a partial picture is being built on the screen. Why is this a fault? Because it means that a procedure can only be defined in terms of already defined procedures (so that, for example, if House calls Triangle, the latter must already be defined or the system will object) and in terms of variables which have already been given values. This confuses the fundamental difference between the *definition* of a procedure and the *call* of a procedure, a difference clearly maintained in all other programming languages. It also demonstrates a lack of understanding of what procedure parameters are for. A pre-release version was distributed with the bizarre warning that 'commands which include the number 79 will do strange things.' It is inconceivable that such errors could arise in a competently designed implementation. It is not possible, either, to shelter under the excuse that these are mere technicalities and that real teachers know what they want. The accompanying manual acknowledges the implementers' debt to Papert's inspirational philosophy. This philosophy emphasises the role of programming in developing problem-solving skills, in particular the use of a top-down strategy for solving problems. The implementation of **Logo Challenge** actually obstructs this strategy (because programs have to be built from the bottom up), and so indicates that the educational philosophy has not been understood either. As confirmation that the development of worthwhile educational software demands an intimate amalgam of educational and computational skills, **Logo Challenge** could hardly be bettered.

In January 1984 the same magazine was able to review some seventy educational software products. With one exception, they follow the established style. The exception, first, is **Edword**,[9] a word-processor designed for pupils to use. Word-processing is one application of computers about which it is difficult to raise any philosophical objections. Even though the publishers are anxious to emphasise that **Edword** was designed by teachers, word-processors have been around long enough for their basic design requirements to be known, as is not the case with most educational software. With MEP support, **Edword** is being published at £60, thus confirming that good educational software will not be cheap. Among the other products reviewed are the usual range: simulations (such as one modelling the flight of NASA's space shuttle); information retrieval systems (such as **Factfile**); games for the home market (such as ones for 4-year-olds, based on the 'Mr Men' characters); and arcade drills (such as **Note Invaders**,[10] in which you shoot down notes or get bombed).

How is it that we come to be eulogising programs of such banality? In the early 1970s the design of educational software was being investigated by a few research groups, including the Computer-Based Learning Project at the University of Leeds, where I was a research student. In 1972 the Project even carried out an investigation of the role of **Logo** in schools. Richard Anderson, now director of the Centre for the Study of Reading at Illinois, gave a seminar in 1972 in which he considered the prospects for writing various kinds of programs before 1977. In particular, he thought it very unlikely that a program could be written to sustain dialogues like that shown in Figure 19.1. I thought this unduly pessimistic and, as I recall, gave a seminar in response the next day in which I explained how it would be done.[11] Of course, I was wrong. We are little nearer today to knowing how to write such a program than we were in 1972. In fact, today nobody seems to think it actually matters that we do not know how to write such programs.

In 1973 the United Kingdom's National Development Programme in Computer-Assisted Learning was launched, and shortly thereafter, coincidentally, I left for a sunnier climate. On my return in 1977 during the last days of the NDP, I was surprised to find a widespread contentment with a large number of smallish programs written in **Basic** and **Fortran**. These two languages had never been mentioned at Leeds as they were patently unsuitable for writing computer-assisted learning programs. The NDP aimed to institutionalise computer-assisted learning, that is, to persuade institutions to continue funding projects after 1977. Thankfully the NDP products never were institutionalised, because they were soon made to look old-fashioned by the arrival of micros with graphics, sound, and so on.

Next came the Micros in Schools scheme (discussed in Chapter 20), and the MEP in 1980. In order to justify the rapid infusion of micros into schools, the MEP has tried to boost the quantity of educational software. Hobson's choice means that this software has to be written as small programs in **Basic** and assembly language. Of course, there is more educational software about, but

Teacher: Which is likely to be colder, Newfoundland or Montana?
Student: Newfoundland.
Please give your reasons for answering Newfoundland.
Newfoundland is further north.
Yes, that's true. Are you arguing then, that if you take any two places in the Northern Hemisphere, the one which is further north will have the lower average temperature?
Yes, I guess so.
I'll tell you now that Montana has lower average temperatures than Newfoundland. Does this fact cause you to change your reasoning?
Yes.
In what way?
Being further north isn't as important as I thought.
Please try to be more precise. Would you, for instance, say that if you take any two places in the Northern Hemisphere, the one furthest south has the colder temperature?
No, I wouldn't say that.
Would you say that how far north a place is has no effect on temperature?
No, I know it has some effect.
Yes, you're right. Distance north does affect temperature. Yet, even though it is further north, Newfoundland has higher average temperatures than Montana. What must this mean?
There must be some other factor.
Yes! Right! What could this factor be?
I don't have any idea.
Why don't you look at your map of North America. Do you see any differences between Montana and Newfoundland?
Montana is in the centre of the country. Newfoundland is on the ocean.
Do you suppose that distance from the ocean affects temperature?
I'm not sure. It would just be a guess.
True! The name for such a guess is an hypothesis. Supposing the hypothesis were correct, what exactly would you predict?
The further a place is from the ocean, the lower the temperature will be.
How could you test your hypothesis?
By comparing temperatures of places different distances from the ocean.
Very good. Let's do that. Suppose we take St Louis, Missouri. Which would be best to compare, Atlanta, Georgia, or Washington DC . . . ?
I would pick Washington.
Why?
Because it's at the same latitude as St Louis.
Why is that important?
Well, if Atlanta were warmer, I wouldn't know whether it was because it was nearer the ocean or further south.

Figure 19.1

I see little evidence that the best examples are any better than those of a decade ago. This should not be surprising, for during the last decade there has been an exclusive emphasis on 'development', with the implication, now fully absorbed by most educational software designers, that everything that needs to be known about the design of effective programs is known and, indeed, there is not much that needs to be known.

Almost all educational software will continue to be written in **Basic** for many years. The largest UK group producing school educational software conceded that they would be 'in trouble' if **Basic** were ever displaced. The expense of rewriting programs and learning new languages is a barrier to progress.

Basic, as we saw in Chapter 12, is such a limiting language that few professional programmers would seriously contemplate using it for a program of any size. Its encouragement of poor programming style makes it particularly unsuitable for young beginners. These deficiencies led to some debate about whether it should be replaced by **Comal**, an extension of **Basic** with extra commands more in tune with modern programming practice.[12] The extensions were so clearly desirable that it is difficult to see what the debate was about: much more radical suggestions would have been more to the point. The outcome has been that the debate has dissolved—we have an improved (but still far from adequate) **Basic**, and **Basic** programmers can now relax and return to their old style of programming.

It is a common mistake to assume that all aspects of the microcomputer revolution are evolving at the same rapid rate. In fact, there has been only a gradual improvement in programming methodology over the last ten years and no breakthrough is foreseeable, for programming is a conceptual skill not a technology. Indeed, the arrival of micros has lowered the average quality of programming, for the mass of micro programmers have to work without the full range of tools available on more powerful computers.

It may be that present programs, like most of those of the NDP, will soon be forgotten as newer technology spreads. A report by the Association of Teachers of Mathematics predicts that 'almost all of the current software will not last through more than one commercial release',[13] new videodisk material making it obsolete.

Perhaps, also, we shall suddenly discover how to write good educational software. The MEP, apparently, can see 'no reason to suppose that a reasonably plentiful supply of software shouldn't be "on tap" within the foreseeable future.'[14] In 1978, Martin[15] had written that

> an outstanding program for computer-aided instruction is a work of great art . . . in the meantime some singularly unstylish programs are being written. Programmers, hurriedly attempting to demonstrate the new machines and infatuated by the ease with which they can make their words appear on the screen, are producing programs as bad as the home movies of an amateur with his first 8mm zoom-lens camera. . . . This is probably a temporary dilemma; teachers rather than programmers are taking over the programming work as the technology spreads.

Strangely, Martin had been able to write exactly the same words in 1970![16]

Regrettably, this 'temporary dilemma' will be with us for many more years: the mould has been cast. Consider for example, the MEP's Microprimer pack, which set out to include 50 programs (for each of the three supported micros) for use in primary schools. These were to be 'trend-setting programs . . . which should ensure a steady flow of good quality software.'[17] The first pack, released in November 1982, contained seven programs: **Litter** and **Animal** (mentioned earlier), a 'shopping simulation', a program based on the toy Bigtrak, a 'diet' program, a pair of programs allowing quizzes to be created, and a program presenting a version of a river-crossing problem. The remaining packs, with 22 programs, maintained this standard. Ten years ago, few people would have thought such programs worth writing: now it is possible to distribute them to every school they become 'trend-setting'.

More distressing, however, than the actual programs is the assumption within the MEP that educational software means no more than such trivial programs. Is it any wonder that the tcps are keen to take up the 'challenge to write to high standards . . . along the lines of these packages'?[18]

Some educational computing enthusiasts are beginning to stagger from the whirligig of hardware change. The chairman of the British Micros and Primary Education group considers that the present choice of three micros for British primary schools is sufficient and pleads for micro manufacturers to develop reliable peripherals rather than new ranges of micros.[17] Not only is this pie in the sky (for a manufacturer who does not produce a new range every two years or so is doomed to bankruptcy) but it reveals a limited vision of the requirements for effective use of computers in schools. Present micros ought to be considered mere prototypes, to be experimented with and discarded as soon as possible. But again, the standards are being set now. I suspect that the present generation of micros will dominate school computing for many more years. For one thing, it is difficult to imagine finance forthcoming to keep school computers up-to-date, especially when decision-makers begin to question the benefits obtained from the present infusion. For another, many schools will lack the enthusiasm to keep on top of rapid technological change. What has yet to be fully appreciated is that computers in schools are not a 'once-in-a-lifetime' event but a continuing commitment. To suggest that teachers will have difficulty sustaining this is no criticism. They simply do not have the time, nor the administrative or technical capacity.

To return to educational software, from where can we hope to gain insights leading to radical improvements in software quality? Braun[2] recognises that 'it is difficult to know how to solve this problem', and can only suggest financial incentives (and this is likely to prove the governmental 'solution'). Ultimately, there can be no solution unless we gain a better understanding of what we are trying to do. Maybe this understanding will develop through the present 'let a thousand weeds bloom' approach. Maybe a concerted research programme into interactive system design and the psychology of human learning and teaching will yield results. There is no guarantee either way.

Some people have argued that a branch of computer science research known as artificial intelligence will lead to improved computer-assisted learning.[19] A bald definition of artificial intelligence is that it is the science of getting computers to do things which would be considered intelligent if done by humans. The aim of the research is to build more useful computers and to understand the nature of intelligence and associated cognitive abilities, such as learning and thinking. It is *not* the aim to implant intelligence in those who may be lacking it, as suggested by Chapman,[20] who wrote in an MEP publication that 'if we can compensate for physical handicaps with artificial limbs, why not compensate for intellectual handicaps with artificial intelligence?'!

A review of a 1982 book on intelligent teaching systems[21] considered that 'this book signals that a whole new era of computer-aided instruction is about to begin.' The chapters in the book were originally published as journal papers in 1979, and many describe work carried out in the early 1970s. Clearly, this new era has been slow to get started. A pessimistic interpretation of artificial intelligence research is that it demonstrates how fundamentally difficult computer-assisted learning actually is. The practical application of artificial intelligence research to computer-assisted learning would demand skill and resources way beyond those used at present to develop educational software. As a result, therefore, most designers will probably continue to regard this research as irrelevant to their needs.

An alternative source of progress is the field of psychology, within which the topic of learning has traditionally been studied. Hawkridge[22] remarks that 'education needs fundamentally new instructional paradigms.' Psychology, however, 'has not yet produced the answers, but it must yield them if we are to take full advantage of this new information technology in education.' But what if psychology does not yield the answers? There is little sign that it will. The conclusion must be that we shall not, in fact, be able to take full advantage of the new information technology in education.

20.   The Influence of Outsiders

It is no longer possible to discuss educational software, the subject of this book, as a pure abstraction. Interests other than the straightforwardly educational are now helping to determine the kind of software which gets written.

Many governments have decided, in the face of the 'all-pervading microcomputer revolution' (as a favourite description puts its), to stimulate the use of computers in education. France, for example, began a national programme in 1971, concentrating first on training teachers in the new technology. In the United States, with its decentralised, largely autonomous state governments, developments have been more patchy. Some states, notably Minnesota and Pennsylvania, have long-established and well-financed educational computing programmes. Japan, too, has greatly expanded its use of computers in education, especially in higher education. Further details of these national schemes can be found in Maddison.[1]

Discounting the National Development Programme in Computer-Assisted Learning, which can charitably be described as a false start, British initiatives began in 1980 with the Department of Industry's Micros in Schools scheme, followed shortly by the Department of Education and Science's Microelectronics Education Programme. (The MEP runs only in England, Wales and Northern Ireland: Scotland has its own programme, the Scottish Microelectronics Development Programme, the SMDP.) It has been remarked upon many times, but is still worth remembering, that the impetus for putting micros in schools came from industrialists and not from educationalists. Under the DoI scheme, secondary schools were offered half the cost of one of two British micros, one of which did not actually exist at the time the scheme was announced. The usual practice in the computer industry is to decide orders on the basis of software provision, not hardware—

especially not hardware that exists only on paper! The scheme has since been extended, in a slightly modified form but still with the patriotic clause, to primary schools, special education schools and teacher training colleges. In addition, similar schemes are being devised for putting toy robots, links to *Prestel*, and perhaps more, into every school. In all, the various schemes has cost the government about £30 million by the end of 1983.

This is not a vast amount by government budget standards to spend in helping children come to terms with a revolution which is supposed to be going to have a dominating effect on their lives, but even so it is reasonable to ask why the money has been spent. If the microcomputer really is 'all-pervading', wouldn't it have pervaded the classroom without any help? The pervasive power of microcomputers has been enormously exaggerated: think through the activities of a normal day and try to imagine how many of them could be significantly altered by computers in whatever form you can imagine them. Many home computer buyers have realised that, far from pervading all their activities, micros can scarcely be found a use at all. But let us accept that it is a government's responsibility not only to react to revolutions but to anticipate them. If it is important for future citizens to know something about computers, then there is a clear case for putting computers in schools now.

Conceding, then, that the primary motivation is a commendable vision of the future needs of society and the individual, are there any fortunate side-effects? First, the government has discovered a relatively cheap source of good publicity. The prime minister is able to claim that, as far as school computing goes, Britain is the most advanced country in the world. In terms of the percentage of schools possessing at least one computer, this may well be true. The fact that few teachers have been trained to make use of the little software available is less tangible. The image that schools are now well endowed with computers has been absorbed by the general public—reinforced, for example, by news bulletins which illustrate any item concerning schools with an irrelevant clip of children pointing at computer screens. It is ironic indeed that the prime minister has chosen to label present schoolchildren as the 'keyboard generation', thereby focusing on the only part of computers which dates from Victorian times and a part which may perhaps be obsolete by the time this generation leaves school.

Building on the visible success of these schemes, the DoI proceeded to use the fact that 'information technology is making an immense contribution to schools' to try to persuade businesses and industries to adopt the new technology. The campaign culminated in advertisements showing children using software like that discussed in this book and asking: 'Is he better equipped to run an office than you are?'

In addition, the three approved British micro manufacturers can now use the large numbers of their products in schools as evidence of their intrinsic worth. Indeed, the DoI schemes have played a notable part in sustaining the indigenous microcomputer industry. The apparent benevolence to the educational system cloaks a multi-million pound subsidy to manufacturers which would have been politically unpalatable if given directly. In 1981, American micros, with their greater software support, were beginning to predominate in British schools. Now they and Japanese micros together, of course, with non-recommended British micros are virtually excluded from British schools—so much for the free market economy! As manufacturers are well aware, the school market is only the thin end of a large wedge. The expectation is that parents will prefer to buy home computers like those used at school, in order to give their children greater access to the educational software which would (they are led to believe) be so successful at school if only it could be used more regularly. Two of the three recommended micros were in fact designed for the home market rather than the educational one.

So, governments and manufacturers have decided that computers are to be used in schools, and, moreover, which computers: what has this to do with educational software? The answer is nothing, and that is precisely the point. From an educational point of view, the main criteria should concern the quality of software available. For an example of the kinds of external problem with which the teacher is now expected to contend, let us consider the **Logo** saga, the provision of the **Logo** language for use on British micros.

Originally, **Logo** was implemented on American main frames in the early 1970s. The first versions on micros were on the Texas

Instruments 99/4A and the Apple II (the latter being delayed because of contractual complications). Imagine a British teacher in 1981 enthused by having just read Papert's book (published in 1980). First he is discouraged from using American micros. He turns instead to the recommended British micros. He reads in October 1981[2] that the 380Z version of **Logo** is 'on its way'. Throughout 1982 its release is promised 'soon'. It is eventually released in April 1983, but is unacceptably slow when drawing (although this is soon remedied). But wait—in the meantime, the 480Z has become the recommended micro. At the time of writing (February 1984), a version for the 480Z has still to be released.

Perhaps instead he read in October 1981 (from the educational manager of the company that manufactures the BBC micro) that the makers of the BBC micro are 'aware of the need for other languages such as . . . **Logo** . . . and they will arrive in due course.'[3] He is assured in May 1982 that it will be ready in September, and again in September that it will be ready in February. At the time of writing, in fact, there is still no sign of a BBC **Logo**.

Or perhaps he read in October 1982[4] of a scheme for obtaining a free copy of **Logo** for the Spectrum. Again, it is promised for March 1983 and . . . to cut a long story short, at the time of writing, its release is still 'imminent'. Regardless of the reasons for these delays, it is surely too much to expect teachers to accept them. Is it any wonder that there is a spate of second-rate, incomplete **Logo** implementations?

It is within this *maelstrom* that the MEP and SMDP have been set up 'to help schools to prepare children for life in which devices and systems based on microelectronics are commonplace and pervasive.'[5] With extensions, the MEP is now set to run until 1986 and to absorb over £20 million of public funds. Bearing in mind the formidable difficulties to be overcome with meagre resources, the achievements of the MEP have been considerable. It originally proposed to support work in three areas: resource organisation and support, teacher training, and curriculum development. Let us take each in turn.

First, it was necessary to set up an infrastructure of regional information centres. Each centre was to be responsible for providing information on hardware and software to schools within its region and, in addition, to exchange information with other regional centres, to form links with local education authorities, to provide some facilities for in-service training, to keep in touch with curriculum development projects, to disseminate software, to organise support for local teachers studying distance learning programmes, and to form links with hardware manufacturers and employers using microelectronics. This is a long list of tasks to be carried out by staff with, inevitably, little or no previous experience. To superimpose such a structure on an already existing educational system required considerable managerial skill. The network of regional centres now exists, but it remains a temporary organisation and therefore one susceptible to changes in government policy.

Regarding teacher training, it is necessary first to appreciate the scale of the problem: of the 400,000 teachers in British schools in 1980 only a very small number had received any kind of computer training whatsoever. In addition, existing computer education was, and still is, a remarkable patchwork that had developed in an *ad hoc* fashion over several years. Most courses were not intended for teachers at all. They ranged from 3-year undergraduate courses, 1-year postgraduate 'conversion' courses, distance learning courses of various kinds from the Open University and elsewhere, diploma and certificate courses run by colleges and polytechnics, various short 'familiarisation' courses run by local authorities and other agencies, training opportunity scheme (TOPS) courses, courses within 'information technology centres' set up by the government, and the BBC's Computer Literacy Project. Amongst all this, or perhaps outside it, the MEP had to arrange acceptable courses for two teachers from each secondary school (and one from each primary school) which wished to take part in the DoI scheme, for this was a condition to be fulfilled by the school.

Between December 1981 and March 1983, the MEP ran courses which yielded 39,145 'teacher day course units', an 'impressive figure [which] illustrates the expanding and progressive direction of teacher training.'[6] Even so, this means that fewer than one teacher in ten had attended as much as a 1-day course. One day a year is quite inadequate to keep up with the rate of technological change, let alone catch up. MEP's courses are distinguished as 'general awareness' courses (of 1–3 days), 'specialist familiarisation' courses (of up to one week), and 'longer specialist' courses (of up to three months). Given the demand for instant knowledge from teachers suddenly faced with using computers in classrooms, it is quite understandable that the emphasis should be on short courses. Unfortunately, the effect has been to imply (and perhaps the MEP directorate has come to believe it) that such short courses are adequate, thus confirming the tcp to-be in his belief that he has mastered all that is relevant to educational computing.

It is in the third area, curriculum development, that the MEP has made least progress. The aim was to develop materials to assist with the teaching and learning of both 'traditional' subjects and new 'information technology' subjects. The MEP, of course, has no direct say in what is done in schools under the guise of computer awareness, computer literacy, computer studies, computer-assisted learning, information technology, or whatever, this being decided by individual headteachers, guided by hidebound examination syllabuses (at least, in secondary schools). But the MEP has courted confusion by not attempting to distinguish clearly between these subjects: they say 'it is evident that "teaching people WITH computers" encompasses, in a proper and important sense, "teaching people ABOUT computers"—i.e. their strengths and limitations.'[7] However, present computer-assisted learning software is quite unlike the bulk of computer software; it is bound to be giving children a distorted view of the strengths and limitations of computers, if that is seriously suggested. The DoI, incidentally, offered no suggestions as to how their computers were to be used, which since they defined computer-assisted learning as 'interactive systems in which the computer "teaches" the pupil by question and answer'[8] is perhaps just as well.

It *is* very difficult to say precisely what should be done in schools in 'computer literacy' and 'computer studies' classes, but this must surely be attempted first. It should be guided by perceptions of future technological developments and by an appreciation of present resources both in equipment and staff. Most importantly, it must be subject to constant revision. It is too difficult a topic to do justice to here. The point of relevance now is that the MEP's reluctance to define the scope of the subject has led to many teachers, fortified by a course of a few days, being able to move into computer studies teaching and to designing educational software.

As regards the development of material for 'traditional' subjects, the prospects for progress would seem more promising. There is a greater concensus on what is to be learned and some twenty years' experience in writing computer-assisted learning software. But first, consider this: in the 1950s, about 90 per cent of computer costs went on hardware with just 10 per cent on software. In the 1980s, the percentages are reversed, 90 per cent of computer costs are now associated with software. Government funding of educational computing reflects the 1950s' proportions, because hardware is a more visible commitment. I can see no reason why school computers should, uniquely, require such cheap software to make adequate use of them. What are the implications for educational finances if, in tune with 1980s reality, it takes £5000 worth of software to support a £500 computer?

In December 1982, the MEP reported that 300 programs had been developed at an average cost of nearly £5000.[9] A year later, 2000–3000 programs were claimed to exist, although we were asked to write off 90 per cent of these as the detritus of teacher training.[10] Being a political organisation, the MEP has to play the 'numbers game' to placate critics. However, such statistics are practically meaningless. In fact, educational software provision is clearly inadequate, in quantity and especially in quality. The MEP has seriously underestimated the finances and, more importantly, the skill and knowledge necessary to develop good-quality software in quantity. The MEP had to move quickly to encourage the development of software to fill the vacuum developed by the DoI scheme. In the longer run, however, it might have been more helpful to say honestly and forcefully that we do not know enough about writing good educational software. The prospects now are that the DoI itself (now the Department of Trade and Industry, the DTI) will intervene to subsidise the fledgling 'educational software industry'. This will, no doubt, boost the quantity of predominantly poor programs, but it seems unlikely than an industrial initiative will seek to fill gaps in fundamental knowledge.

The government's information technology initiatives, in particular, the 'micros in schools' policy, clearly have widespread public support. Without it, the unprecedented attempt to change educational policies and practices would not have been accepted so willingly. None the less, it is a precedent and one which, with the increasing rate of change in technology, is likely to be followed from now on. We are entitled to fear that these initiatives will be influenced by short-term political objectives rather than by a clear vision of the needs of future society and individuals, and what needs to be done now to satisfy them.

PART 5

Conclusion

21. Conclusions

Educational software matters. It will only be through good educational software that the increasingly wonderful educational hardware will be made to work. It seems likely that pupils will spend a fair proportion of their time interacting with educational software. Educational software is important enough to warrant the applications of whatever skills, knowledge and experience we can muster.

The widespread belief that we already have good educational software or, if not, that it is just round the corner, seems to me to be entirely unfounded. Even the software which at a first glance seems quite impressive is sadly deficient when looked at closely. It is time that educational software designers stopped deluding themselves and their customers: the design of educational software is extraordinarily difficult. We cannot expect good products to materialise by improvised hackery that flies in the face of standard educational psychology and software design principles.

This book should not be interpreted as a 'back to the blackboard' call: 'back to the drawing-board' maybe, but there is clearly already a role for computers in education. Present micros can be used to provide a general 'computer awareness' for pupils, although rather more thought must be given to what this should involve. They may also support 'computer studies' courses, as indeed most of today's micros do, in practice. Computers may also be used to help with routine tasks such as word-processing, record-keeping, statistical computations, and so on. But the case for computer-assisted learning using present software seems very weak.

To suggest a return to the drawing-board is to suggest a need for more fundamental research. Practising teachers have a healthy scepticism about so-called 'research'. However, most of what is best about present educational computing is the product of many years' research, not the product of a cottage educational software industry. For example, **Logo** (one of the few redeeming features on a bleak landscape) was inspired by Piaget's life-long research on developmental psychology, was designed at a private research establishment in the late 1960s and was then fostered for several years in artificial intelligence research laboratories. As I have argued at length elsewhere, the subject of artificial intelligence remains the most promising source of new ideas for educational software. The fact that there are today so few products from research in evidence is not altogether the fault of researchers: support for such research over the last decade has been paltry. There is very little research now being carried out to complement the expenditure on educational hardware, and almost no longer-term research.

This is not just a plea for more computing research, for I have no doubt that the educational problems are even more difficult. In this book, I have concentrated on the question of whether software is technically good, rather than on whether it is educationally effective. This is partly because I know more about the former and also because there has been shamefully little attempt to discover the extent to which present educational software is effective. While the United Kingdom government can spend £30–50 million on putting computer hardware into schools, the Research Councils are struggling to raise £500,000 to support related research. It is unrealistic to expect teachers in the classroom to do research evaluating educational software.

Those teachers who have most enthusiastically taken up educational computing have on the whole (of course, there are exceptions) mistaken the acquisition of superficial skills for the mastery of a well-established discipline. The lack of computing expertise is understandable in newcomers to the scene, but what is hard to accept is the insistence that there is no more to computer science and, if there were, it would be irrelevant anyway. Even stranger is the neglect of sound educational principles which seems to follow once the new technology is taken up.

My criticisms of some of the activities of the teacher-cum-programmers should not be taken as a general criticism of teachers. I have every sympathy and respect for teachers striving to make computers work in their classrooms. The majority of teachers have deep doubts about the role of computers in education, but there is some reluctance to voice these doubts. This is partly because they fear that their doubts are without foundation but are a result of their own ignorance of computer technology. The national commitment to teacher training and updating seems half-hearted. If we are serious, we need to consider radical changes, for example, to expect every teacher to spend his sixth year, say, on courses to update his skills and knowledge, of educational theory as well as technology: anything less and we are bound to continue to muddle and to struggle.

The present lack of understanding of the new technology leads to an atmosphere in which educators, while not necessarily besotted with the highly esteemed hardware, are nevertheless eager to interpret its use as validating educational ideas which in fact should be subjected to deep and critical scrutiny. The computer as *deus ex machina* has caused the consideration of educational processes to be postponed. It is to be hoped that the inadequacies of educational software will eventually lead to a reassessment of educational aims.

Many futurologists are convinced that computers will inevitably infiltrate the professions, including education, taking over many of the activities presently carried out by trained experts. However, it is not inevitable that computers will be widely used to aid learning, nor that they will be used to good effect in education. If computers cannot be made to enhance the quality of education we have the choice not to use them. We must bear in mind that the style of computer interactions has a social conditioning role outside the explicit educational content of the software.

Many of the present signs are not encouraging, as the preceding pages indicate. However, one must remain optimistic that, in the long run, the necessary changes in the balance of activities will occur and that an effective role for the computer as a learning aid will be developed. Let us hope that it is not a longer run than even I am prepared for.

Notes

Chapter 1

1. **Climate** is available from Heinemann Computers in Education Ltd, cost £12 (prices quoted in this book are approximate).

Chapter 2

1. R.G. Barry and R.J. Chorley, *Atmosphere, Weather and Climate*, 4th edn (Bungay: Metheun, 1982), pp. 366–8.
2. *Computing*, 3 March 1983, p. 32.
3. Paul. H. Hirst, 'What is teaching?', *Journal of Curriculum Studies*, **3**, 1 (1971), 5–18.
4. *Computers in Schools*, **5**, 4 (1983), p. 121.
5. MUSE Report No. 4, 'Educational software', (December 1983), p. 18.
6. Joseph Day, 'A successful science trio', *Educational Computing*, **4**, 9 (1983), p. 17.
7. Comments made during an interview at Plymouth in November 1982.

Chapter 3

1. This excludes the human teacher from the class of media, as recommended by A.A. Lumsdaine, 'Instruments and media of instruction', in *Handbook of Research on Teaching*, ed. N.L. Gage (Chicago: Rand McNally, 1963), pp. 583–682.
2. Derek Rowntree, *Educational Technology in Curriculum Development* (London: Harper & Row, 1982), pp. 114–22.
3. R.W. Kulhavy, 'Feedback in written instruction', *Review of Educational Research*, **50** (1977), 211–32.
4. John Maddison, *Education in the Microelectronics Era* (Milton Keynes: Open University Press, 1983), p. 97.
5. For example, **Superhangman** (from IJK Software, cost £4) plays 'Land of Hope and Glory' or 'The Death March' at the end of each game.

Chapter 4

1. **Lost Dutchman's Gold** is available from The Programmer's Guild.
2. Bob Liddil, 'On the road to adventure', *Byte*, **5**, 12 (1980), 158–70.
3. Daniel Chandler, 'Great expectations', *Educational Computing*, **3**, 9 (1982), 24–5.
4. Antony Mullan, 'Infant words and a sense of adventure', *Educational Computing*, **2**, 12 (1981), 49–51.
5. Anon., 'Have you had an adventure lately?' *Educational Computing*, **4**, 9 (1983), 28–9.
6. **The Hobbit** is available from Melbourne House, cost £15.
7. *Educational Computing*, **4**, 9 (1983), p. 31.
8. James A. Levin and Yaakov Kareev, 'Personal computers and education: the challenge to schools', CHIP Report 98 (Center for Human Information Processing, University of California, San Diego, 1980), pp. 32–8.

Chapter 5

1. **Hunt the Thimble** is available from Ginn Microcomputer Software, cost £17.
2. **Saqqara** is available from Ginn Microcomputer Software, cost £32.
3. Barry Holmes and Ian Whittington, 'Simulations—the creative use of resources', *Micro-scope*, **5** (1982), 10–12.
4. **Inkosi** is available from Chalksoft, cost £6.
5. **Tourism** is available from Thomas Nelson Ltd, cost £22.
6. **Mary Rose** is available from Ginn Microcomputer Software, cost £32.
7. **Newsagent** and **DVLC** are available from ICL/CES, cost £4.
8. According to the Addison-Wesley advertisement for the UMIST packages.
9. **Newton** is available from Edward Arnold Ltd, cost £13.
10. J.S. Bruner and D.R. Olson, 'Learning through experience and learning through media', *Prospects*, **1** (1973), 20–38.
11. **GB Ltd** is available from Simon W. Hessel, cost £6.
12. **Litter** is distributed by MEP as part of Microprimer Pack 1.

Chapter 6

1. A. Payne, B. Hutchings and P. Ayre, *Computer Software for Schools* (London: Pitman, 1980), pp. 13–48.
2. **World War One** is available from Sussex Publications Ltd, cost £17.
3. John Goodlad, John O'Toole, Jr and Louise Tyler, *Computers and Information Systems in Education* (New York: Harcourt, Brace & World, 1966), pp. 14–16.
4. Christopher Smith, 'Revision programs for biology', *Educational Computing*, **4**, 2 (1983), 31.

5. Ronnie Goldstein, 'SMILE and the micro', *Mathematics Teaching*, **101** (1982), 25–9.
6. **Barset** is one of fourteen programs in the Micros in the Mathematics Classroom pack available from Longman Micro Software, cost £25.
7. **Janeplus** is available from Longman Micro Software, cost £12.
8. John Anderson, Foreword to *Selected Readings in Computer-Based Learning*, ed. Nick Rushby (London: Kogan Page, 1981), p. 8.
9. Alan Maddison, *Microcomputers in the Classroom* (London: Hodder & Stoughton, 1982), pp. 96–8.

Chapter 7

1. Ken Tait, Roger Hartley and Richard Anderson, 'Feedback procedures in computer-assisted arithmetic instruction', *British Journal of Educational Psychology*, **43** (1973), 161–71.
2. **Factfile** is available from Cambridge University Press, cost £15. Also distributed in the MEP Microprimer Pack 1.
3. **Leep** is produced by the Inner London Education Authority Computer Service.
4. **Questd** is available from Chiltern Computing.
5. **Sir** was developed by the British Library: see *Calnews* **21** (1983), p. 7.
6. J. Richard Ennals, *Beginning Micro-Prolog* (Chichester: Ellis Horwood, 1983), pp. 128–32.
7. Paul H. Hirst, 'Liberal education and the nature of education', in *Philosophical Analysis and Education*, ed. R.D. Archambault (London: Routledge & Kegan Paul, 1965), pp. 113–38.
8. William Paisley, 'Information and work', in *Progress in Communication Sciences*, Vol. II, ed. Brenda Dervin and Melvin J. Voigt (Norwood, NJ: Ablex Publishing, 1980).
9. Daniel Bell, 'The social framework of the information society', in *The Microelectronics Revolution*, ed. Tom Forester (Oxford: Blackwell, 1980).

Chapter 8

1. Alan Lesgold, paper presented at a Conference on Microcomputers in Education: Cognitive and Social Design Principles held at the University of California, San Diego, 1981.
2. **Percents** is published by LCL, cost £7 (including three other programs).
3. For example, an exercise on reading micrometers and verniers, one of nine programs of a physics set, available from MUSE, cost £6.
4. **Trains** is included in the MEP Microprimer Pack 2 (originally from Newman College).
5. **Claws** is available from Bryants, cost £4.

6. **Bomber** is available from Fisher-Marriott Software, cost £6.
7. Les McLean, 'A cut above the majority', *Educational Computing*, **4**, 2 (1983), 15.
8. **Number Gulper** is available from Applied Systems Knowledge, cost £10.
9. **Bertie** is available from Dartmouth College.

Chapter 9

1. Patrick Suppes, 'Current trends in computer-assisted instruction', in *Advances in Computers 18*, ed. M.C. Yovits (New York: Academic Press, 1979).
2. Peter Ayscough, '**Calchem** reaches 50', *Calnews*, **21** (1983), 1–2.
3. WICAT Systems, Inc., 'WICAT Training Systems', internal report (1983).
4. Alan Maddison, *Microcomputers in the Classroom* (London: Hodder & Stoughton, 1982, p. 151.

Chapter 10

1. **Translate** is available from ESM, cost £6.
2. R.W. Lawler, 'Designing computer-based microworlds', *Byte*, **7**, 8 (1982), 138–60.
3. W. Feurzeig, S. Papert, M. Bloom, R. Grant and C. Solomon, 'Programming languages as a conceptual framework for teaching mathematics', *Report No. 1899* (Cambridge, Mass.: Bolt Beranek and Newman, Inc., 1969).
4. J.A.M. Howe, T. O'Shea and F. Plane, 'Teaching mathematics through **Logo** programming: an evaluation study', in *Computer Assisted Learning: Scope, Progress and Limits*, ed. R. Lewis and E.D. Tagg (Amsterdam: North-Holland, 1980).
5. E. Paul Goldenberg, '**Logo**—a cultural glossary', *Byte*, **7**, 8 (1982), 210–28.
6. S. Papert, D. Watt, A. diSessa and S. Weir, 'Final report of the Brookline **Logo** project', *Logo Memo No. 53* (Cambridge, Mass.: MIT AI Lab., 1979).
7. Seymour Papert, *Mindstorms: Children, Computers and Powerful Ideas* (New York: Basic Books, 1980), p. 5.
8. Cynthia Solomon, 'Teaching young children to program in a **Logo** turtle computer culture', *SIGCUE Bulletin*, **12**, 3 (1978), 20–9.
9. Colin Terry, '**Logo**', *Educational Computing*, **5**, 1 (1984), p. 19.
10. See, for example, Aaron Sloman, *The Computer Revolution in Philosophy* (Brighton: Harvester, 1979).
11. Cynthia Solomon, 'Introducing **Logo** to children', *Byte,* **7**, 8 (1982), 196–208.
12. Piet Hien, *Grooks* (Cambridge, Mass.: MIT Press, 1966), p. 34.
13. Seymour Papert, 'New cultures from new technologies', *Byte,* **5**, 9 (1980), 230–40.

Chapter 11

1. Glenford J. Myers, *The Art of Software Testing* (New York: John Wiley, 1979).
2. David Gries, *The Science of Programming* (Berlin: Springer, 1981).
3. Mike Bawtree, 'Consider the binomial theorem . . .', *Educational Computing*, **2,** 9 (1981), 36.
4. Frank Bell, 'Home-grown programs enliven the laboratory', *Educational Computing*, **3,** 5 (1982), 30–1.
5. William A. Wulf, Mary Shaw, Paul N. Hilfinger and Lawrence Flon, *Fundamental Structures of Computer Science* (Reading, Mass.: Addison-Wesley, 1981).
6. Peter Naur and Brian Randell (eds), 'Software engineering. Report on a conference sponsored by the NATO Science Committee, Germany, October 1968', (Brussels: NATO Scientific Affairs Division, 1969).
7. Niklaus Wirth, *Algorithms + Data Structures = Programs* (Englewood Cliffs, NJ: Prentice-Hall, 1976).
8. Ruth Poulton, **'Animal'**, in *Five of the Best*, ed. Ron Jones (London: Council for Educational Technology, 1982).
9. Jon Coupland, 'Software: an historical overview', in *Exploring English with Microcomputers*, ed. Daniel Chandler (London: Council for Educational Technology, 1983).
10. Clark Weissman, **Lisp 1.5** *Primer* (Belmont, Calif.: Dickenson, 1967).
11. Niklaus Wirth, 'Program development by stepwise refinement', *Communications ACM*, **14** (1971), 221–7.

Chapter 12

1. Saul Alagic and Michael A. Arbib, *The Design of Well-Structured and Correct Programs* (New York: Springer-Verlag, 1978).
2. John Backus, 'Can programming be liberated from the von Neumann style?', *Communication ACM*, **21** (1978), 613–41.
3. Bob Lewis, 'Computer simulation of science laboratory experiments', *Bulletin of the Institute of Mathematics and its Applications*, **7,** 8 (1971).
4. Seymour Papert, *Mindstorms: Children, Computers and Powerful Ideas* (New York: Basic Books, 1980), pp. 32–4.
5. Jan Noyes, 'The QWERTY keyboard: a review', *International Journal of Man-Machine Studies*, **18** (1983), 265–81.
6. Chris A. Butlin, letter, 'Schools council and TRS–80', *Computers in Schools*, **4,** 1 (1981) p. 32.
7. Thomas E. Kurtz, 'On the way to standard **Basic**', *Byte*, **7,** 6 (1982), 182–218.
8. Colin Wells, *Aspects of Programming for Teaching Unit Design and Development* (London: Council for Educational Technology, 1983).
9. Ron Jones, *Microcomputers – their Uses in Primary Schools* (London: Council for Educational Technology, 1980), p. 14.

10. Jim Seth, 'A status report from the Far West', *Educational Computing*, **3**, 7 (1982), p. 14.
11. Brian Harvey, 'Why **Logo**?', *Byte*, **7**, 8 (1982), 163–93.
12. Ben Wegbreit, *Studies in Extensible Programming Languages* (New York: Garland, 1980).
13. J. Richard Ennals, 'Logic as a computer language', *Micro-scope*, **6** (1982), p. 9.
14. J. Richard Ennals, '**Prolog** can link diverse subjects with logic and fun', *Practical Computing*, **4**, 3 (1981), p. 92.
15. Steven Hardy, 'Towards more natural programming languages', Working Paper, Cognitive Studies Programme (University of Sussex, 1982).
16. J. Richard Ennals, *Beginning* **Micro-Prolog** (Chichester: Ellis Horwood, 1983), p. 145.
17. Bill Tallon, Derek Ball and David Tomley, '**Basic** or **Prolog**: Choosing the right language for a biology teaching task', *Computers in Schools*, **5**, 1 (1982), 21–3.
18. J. Richard Ennals, 'Logic as a computer language', *Micro-scope*, **6** (1982), p. 9.
19. M. Wertheimer, *Productive Thinking* (New York: Harper & Row, 1959).

Chapter 13

1. John A. Starkweather, 'A common language for a variety of conversational programming needs', in *Computer-Assisted Instruction*, ed. Richard C. Atkinson and H.A. Wilson (New York: Academic Press, 1969).
2. Stewart Denenberg, 'A personal evaluation of the PLATO system', *Sigcue Bulletin*, **12**, 2 (1978), 3–10.
3. PLATO and TICCIT (see subsequently) are two large-scale US computer-assisted learning projects. For a summary of these projects, see Tim O'Shea and John Self, *Learning and Teaching with Computers* (Brighton: Harvester, 1983), 86–98.
4. R.A. Avner, 'Longitudinal studies in computer-based authoring', in *Issues in Instructional System Development*, ed. Harold F. O'Neil, Jr (New York: Academic Press, 1979).
5. Peter Ayscough, '**Staf** author guide', Report ICCC/UG9 (Imperial College Computer Centre, London, 1981).
6. M.D. Merrill, E. Schneider and K. Fletcher, *TICCIT* (Englewood Cliffs, NJ: Educational Technology Publications, 1980).
7. Tim Teitelbaum and Thomas Reps, 'The Cornell program synthesizer: a syntax-directed programming environment', *Communication ACM*, **24** (1981), 563–73.
8. Greg Kearsley, 'Authoring systems in computer-based education', *Communications ACM*, **25** (1982), 429–37.
9. WICAT Systems Inc., 'WICAT training systems', Internal Report (1983).

Chapter 14

1. W.J. Hansen, 'User engineering principles for interactive systems', *Proceedings of the Fall Jt. Computer Conference*, **39** (Montvale, N.J.: AFIPS Press, 1971), 523–32.
2. Ben Shneiderman, *Software Psychology: Human Factors in Computer and Information Systems* (Cambridge, Mass.: Winthrop, 1980).
3. Charles Sweeten, 'Guidelines for educational software', (Micro Users in Secondary Education group, 1981).
4. C. Unger (ed.), *Command Languages* (Amsterdam: North-Holland, 1975).
5. Thomas P. Moran, 'The command language grammar: a representation for the user interface of interactive computer systems', *International Journal of Man–Machine Studies,* **15** (1981), 3–50.
6. D.L. Want, 'Keyword-driven interaction in computer-assisted learning', in *Involving Micros in Education*, ed. R. Lewis and E.D. Tagg (Amsterdam: North-Holland, 1982).
7. Phyllis Reisner, 'Using a formal grammar in human factors design of an interactive graphics system', *IEEE Transactions on Software Engineering,* **7** (1981), 229–40.
8. Robert J.K. Jacob, 'Using formal specifications in the design of a human–computer interface', *Communications ACM*, **26** (1983), 259–64.
9. David C. Smith, Charles Irby, Ralph Kimball and Eric Harslem, 'The star user interface: an overview', in *AFIPS Conference Proceedings* (Arlington, VA.: AFIPS Press, 1982), 515–28.
10. Thomas Green, 'Learning big and little programming languages', in *Classroom Computers and Cognitive Science*, ed. Alex Cherry Wilkinson (New York: Academic Press, 1983).
11. J. Abbot, *Man/Machine Interface Design* (Chichester: John Wiley, 1983).

Chapter 15

1. Deryn Watson, 'Some implications of micros on curriculum development', in *Involving Micros in Education*, ed. R. Lewis and E.D. Tagg (Amsterdam: North-Holland, 1982).
2. Hugh Burkhardt, Rosemary Fraser, Max Clowes, Jim Eggleston and Colin Wells, *Design and Development of Programs as Teaching Material* (London: Council for Educational Technology, 1983).
3. Douglas B. Lenat, Alan Borning, David McDonald, Craig Taylor and Stephen Weyer, 'Knoesphere: building expert systems with encyclopedic knowledge', *Proceedings of the 8th International Jt. Conference on Artificial Intelligence* (Los Altos, Calif.: William Kaufmann, Inc., 1983).

Chapter 16

1. M. Johnstone, 'What makes a good program?', *Micro-scope*, **7** (1982), 21–2.
2. Russell Jones, 'Thoroughly modern Collins', *Computing*, **11**, 32 (1983), p. 27.
3. I.D. Hill and B.L. Meek (eds), *Programming Language Standardisation* (New York: Halstead Press, 1980).
4. Peter J.L. Wallis, 'The preparation of guidelines for portable programming in high-level languages', *Computer Journal*, **25** (1982), 375–8.

Chapter 17

1. Lewis Mumford, *The Myth of the Machine: Technics and Development* (New York: Harcourt Brace, 1966).
2. Marianne Amarel, 'The classroom: an instructional setting for teachers, students, and the computer', in *Classroom Computers and Cognitive Science*, ed. Alex Cherry Wilkinson (New York: Academic Press, 1983).
3. Michael Bawtree, 'Effects of IT on the teaching environment', *Educational Computing*, **4**, 1 (1983), 32–3.
4. Herbert Simon, 'The shape of automation', in *Management and Corporations, 1985*, ed. M.L. Anshen and G.L. Bach (New York: McGraw-Hill, 1960).
5. William E. Drake, *Intellectual Foundations of Modern Education* (Columbus, Ohio: Charles E. Merrill, 1967), p. 273.
6. Joseph Weizenbaum, *Computer Power and Human Reason* (San Francisco: W.H. Freeman, 1976).

Chapter 18

1. Bryan Spielman, Editorial, *Computers in Schools*, **3**, 4 (1981).
2. Alan Hill, 'The World Conference at Lausanne', *Computers in Schools*, **4**, 1 (1981), 18–20.
3. Roger Keeling, 'The next steps', *Micro-scope*, **7** (1982), 2.
4. Derek Rowntree, *Educational Technology in Curriculum Development* (London: Harper & Row, 1974), p. 4.
5. Gregg Williams, 'The new generation of human-engineered software', *Byte*, **8**, 4 (1983), 6–7.
6. Helen Smith, **'Spell'**, *Micro-scope*, **7** (1982), 26–7.
7. R.C. Atkinson and D.N. Hansen, 'Computer-assisted instruction in initial reading: the Stanford project', *Reading Research Quarterly*, **2** (1966), 5–25.
8. Bryan Spielman, 'Scratchpad', *Computers in Schools*, **4**, 1 (1981), p. 3.
9. Daniel Chandler, *Exploring English with Microcomputers* (London: Council for Educational Technology, 1983), p. 6.
10. Ian Black, 'Software evaluation', *Micro-scope*, **7** (1982), 19.

11. Derek Hayes, 'Programming in **Pascal**', *Educational Computing*, **4**, 3 (1983), 23.
12. Derrick Daines, 'We live in critical times', *Educational Computing*, **4**, 6 (1983), 22.

Chapter 19

1. Peter Coburn, Peter Kelman, Nancy Roberts, Thomas Snyder, Daniel Watt and Cheryl Weiner, *Practical Guide to Computers in Education* (Reading, Mass.: Addison-Wesley, 1982), p. 113.
2. Ludwig Braun, 'Computer-aided learning and the microcomputer revolution', *Programmed Learning and Educational Technology*, **18** (1981), 223–9.
3. David Hawkridge, *New Information Technology in Education* (London: Croom Helm, 1983), p. 142.
4. John Maddison, *Education in the Microelectronics Era* (Milton Keynes: Open University Press, 1983), p. 87.
5. Derrick Daines, 'We live in critical times', *Educational Computing*, **4**, 6 (1983), 22.
6. Gary D. Borich and Ron P. Jemelka, *Programs and Systems: an Evaluation Perspective* (New York: Academic Press, 1981).
7. **Logo Challenge** is available from Addison-Wesley, cost £30.
8. *Computers in Schools*, **6**, 1 (1983), p. 25.
9. **Edword** is available from Clwyd Technics, cost £60.
10. **Note Invaders** is available from Chalksoft, cost £9.
11. John Self, 'Student models in computer-aided instruction', *International Journal of Man-Machine Studies,* **6** (1974), 261–76.
12. Roy Atherton, *Structured Programming in Comal* (Chichester: Ellis Horwood, 1982).
13. Association of Teachers of Mathematics, *Working Notes on Microcomputers in Mathematical Education* (Derby: ATM, 1983), p. 28.
14. MEP information sheet on 'Microcomputers in Primary Education' (1982), p. 5.
15. James Martin, *The Wired Society* (Englewood Cliffs, NJ: Prentice-Hall, 1978), p. 232.
16. James Martin and Adrian Norman, *The Computerized Society* (Englewood Cliffs, NJ: Prentice-Hall, 1970), p. 129.
17. Ron Jones, 'MAPE matters', *Micro-scope,* **6** (1982), 24–5.
18. Ron Jones, 'MAPE matters', *Micro-scope,* **7** (1982), 14–15.
19. Tim O'Shea and John Self, *Learning and Teaching with Computers* (Brighton: Harvester, 1983).
20. Bryan Chapman, 'Problems, perspectives, paradoxes, possibilities', *Curriculum Comment*, **1** (1983), 2–3.
21. Derek Sleeman and John Seely Brown, *Intelligent Teaching Systems* (New York: Academic Press, 1982).
22. David Hawkridge, *New Information Technology in Education* (London: Croom Helm, 1983), p. 211.

Chapter 20

1. John Maddison, *Education in the Microelectronics Era* (Milton Keynes: Open University Press, 1983).
2. Michael Thorne, 'Programming and learning', *Computers in Schools*, **4**, 2 (1981), 25–30.
3. John Coll, 'The BBC microcomputer', *Computers in Schools*, **4**, 1 (1981), 17–18.
4. *Educational Computing*, **3**, 8 (1982), p. 10.
5. Richard Fothergill and John Anderson, 'Strategy for the microelectronics programme (MEP)', *Programmed Learning and Educational Technology*, **18** (1981), 121–9.
6. Lynn Craig, 'MEP INSET activities to date', *Educational Computing*, **4**, 7 (1983), p. 25.
7. MEP information sheet on 'Microcomputers in Primary Education' (1982), p. 3.
8. Department of Industry, *Information Technology: the Age of Electronic Information* (London: DoI, 1981).
9. *Educational Computing*, **3**, 7 (1982), p. 8.
10. John Anderson, 'The teacher and the researcher—who pays the ferryman?', SSRC Workshop on Micros in Education (November 1983).

Index